PUFFIN BOOKS
GAUTAMA BUDDHA

Rohini Chowdhury writes for both children and adults and has more than twenty books and several short stories to her credit. Her published writing is in both Hindi and English, and covers a wide spectrum of literary genres including translations, novels, short fiction, comics and non-fiction. Her most recent publication is the translation of the seventeenth-century Braj Bhasha text *Ardhakathanak*, widely regarded as the first autobiography in an Indian language, into modern Hindi and into English. Her first short story, *Kosi*, won the runner-up in the New Writer Prose and Poetry Prizes, 2001, in the UK. Her interests include translation, mythology, folklore, mathematics and history. Her forthcoming works include an exploration of mathematics in India from ancient times to the modern, and a translation of the Hindi novel *Tyagpatra* by Jainendra, into English. She also runs a story website at www.longlongtimeago.com.

Rohini's professional experience prior to moving into the writing and technology space was as a strategy consultant for five years. She holds a PGDM from the Indian Institute of Management, Ahmedabad, and an Honours degree in Economics from Jadavpur University, Kolkata.

Other books in the *Puffin Lives* series

Mother Teresa: Apostle of Love
by Rukmini Chawla
Jawaharlal Nehru: The Jewel of India
by Aditi De
Ashoka: The Great and Compassionate King
by Subhadra Sen Gupta
Rani Lakshmibai: The Valiant Queen of Jhansi
by Deepa Agarwal
Akbar: The Mighty Emperor
by Kavitha Mandana
Mahatma Gandhi: The Father of the Nation
by Subhadra Sen Gupta
Subhas Chandra Bose: The Great Freedom Fighter
by Anu Kumar
Guru Nanak: The Enlightened Master
by Sreelata Menon
Swami Vivekananda: A Man with a Vision
by Devika Rangachari
The 14th Dalai Lama: Buddha of Compassion
by Aravinda Anantharaman

GAUTAMA
Buddha
LORD OF WISDOM

ROHINI CHOWDHURY

PUFFIN BOOKS
An imprint of Penguin Random House

PUFFIN BOOKS

USA | Canada | UK | Ireland | Australia
New Zealand | India | South Africa | China

Puffin Books is part of the Penguin Random House group of companies
whose addresses can be found at global.penguinrandomhouse.com

Published by Penguin Random House India Pvt. Ltd
4th Floor, Capital Tower 1, MG Road,
Gurugram 122 002, Haryana, India

Penguin
Random House
India

First published in Puffin by Penguin Books India 2011

Text copyright © Rohini Chowdhury 2011
Map and Illustrations copyright © Penguin Books India 2011

ISBN 9780143331773

Typeset in Bembo by Eleven Arts, Delhi

Printed at Repro India Limited

www.penguin.co.in

✿ Acknowledgements

I would like to thank Stephen Batchelor for his unstinting generosity in allowing me to use his book *Confessions of a Buddhist Atheist* as a reference source for this book. I would also like to say a big thank you to Sudeshna Shome Ghosh of Puffin India, who made this book possible.

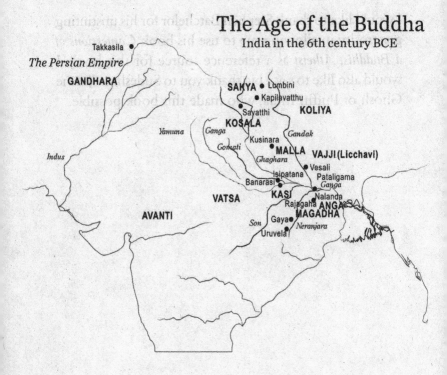

The Age of the Buddha
India in the 6th century BCE

The Persian Empire

Takkasila

GANDHARA

Indus

Yamuna

Ganga

Gomati

SAKYA • Lumbini
  • Kapilavatthu
  • Sayatthi

KOSALA

Kusinara • MALLA

Ghaghara

Gandak

KOLIYA

VAJJI (Licchavi)

• Vesali

Isipatana • Pataligama

Banarasi • *Ganga*

KASI • Nalanda

VATSA

AVANTI

Son

Gaya • MAGADHA
Rajagaha ANGA

Uruvela *Neranjara*

Contents

1 🪷 Reconstructing Buddha

Even though he was one of the most influential men who ever walked the earth, very little is known about the life of Siddhartha Gautama, the man we call the Buddha. His teachings were followed for 1,500 years in India, and became the guiding principles of life for both rich and poor, high born and low-caste. Men and women from all walks of life followed the path he showed. From India his teachings spread to Tibet, Sri Lanka, South-east Asia, Korea, Japan, China and Central Asia, so that more than half of humanity came into its fold. His teachings form the core of the religion known today as Buddhism, and are still followed by almost 400 million people around the world. Given that his teachings led to one of the world's most extraordinary religious and cultural movements, it is both ironic and frustrating that we know almost nothing about him, and what we do know has to be gleaned from scattered references in Buddhist texts and scriptures.

One reason for this lack of information is the Buddha himself. The Buddha believed that no man should be revered above another, for to do so would distract one from the path to enlightenment. He did not allow anyone, including his disciples, to worship him—it was not his life that was important, but his teachings. As a result, even the Buddhist scriptures contain very little about his life. The first historical mention of Buddhism occurs in the inscriptions of King Ashoka, who ruled India from 269 to 232 BCE, some two hundred years after the Buddha's death. This lack of information led Western scholars in the nineteenth century to question the existence of the Buddha as a real, historical person. But modern re-readings of the Buddhist scriptures show beyond a doubt that the Buddha did exist. It is now most commonly accepted that Siddhartha Gautama was born in 563 BCE and died at the age of eighty in 483 BCE.

The Buddhist scriptures, scanty in detail though they are, remain our best source of information about him. They consist of a huge number of texts compiled after the Buddha's death; many of these texts are in the local language of the region or country in which they were composed—Tibetan, Chinese, Burmese and so on. The oldest texts are in Pali, an ancient form of spoken Sanskrit once used in northern India. These texts, which are generally referred to as the Pali Canon, are considered by scholars to be the most useful when trying to understand the life of the Buddha.

The Pali Canon was composed very soon after the Buddha's death, upon the initiative of the monk Mahakashyapa, his chief disciple. The Buddha passed away in the small north Indian town of Kushinagara. As the funeral flames burnt away the Buddha's mortal remains, his monks had been overcome with grief, and kings and princes had threatened to go to war with each other for the honour of possessing his ashes. Only Mahakashyapa had remained clear-eyed and calm. He had told the grieving monks, 'The Buddha is now cremated, but we are not concerned with his relics—kings, ministers, the rich, and all his lay followers will preserve them and do them honour. Our concern is with his teachings. We must collect all his sayings, so that we can pass them on to future generations. We must not allow the world to say that now that the Buddha is no more, his word too has vanished like the smoke.' And he had called upon the monks to gather together at the Satpanni Cave in Rajagriha, the capital city of the powerful kingdom of Magadha in northern India. This gathering is known to history as the First Buddhist Council. The Council had the support of Ajatashatru, Magadha's strong and dynamic ruler, and a follower of the Buddha.

At the Council, the Buddha's teachings, which had been committed to memory by his disciples, were recited, verified and classified. The texts were set in verses such as the Buddha himself may have used, in a style that involved much repetition, and this made the texts easier to remember. The texts were then memorized by the monks and passed down orally through the centuries. This compilation is known as the Pali Canon. Its oral transmission through the ages is considered to be remarkably accurate, despite the changes and modifications that would have occurred through the years. About a hundred years after the Buddha's death, the Second Buddhist Council was held. It is believed that by this time the texts of the Pali Canon had reached the form in which they are available to us today. The Pali Canon was finally written down in the first century BCE, in Sri Lanka.

The story of Siddhartha Gautama, as told in the Buddhist tradition, is familiar to many of us. It is the story of a spoilt young man, the son of a king, who lived in luxury, quite unaware of life's miseries. One day, while outside the palace walls, he saw a sick man, an old man, a corpse, and a monk. These four sights so shocked him that he gave up his life of luxury, became a monk, and after six years of penance attained enlightenment and became a Buddha. He then spent the rest of his life as a monk, wandering from place to place, preaching his path to enlightenment. He died at the age of eighty, having reached Nirvana, or freedom from the cycle of birth and rebirth.

Interestingly, the Pali Canon tells a story that is quite different in its details. Gautama's father is not a king, but a relatively minor vassal of the king of Kosala. The story of the four sights, though told by the Buddha himself in one of his discourses, is part of the story of another Buddha called Vipassi, who lived long before Gautama. Today we use the term 'the Buddha' to refer exclusively to the historical Siddhartha Gautama, but in ancient India 'Buddha' was a title given to anyone who attained enlightenment, and by his knowledge of the absolute Truth, became superior to all beings, human and divine. According to Buddhist tradition there have been twenty-five such beings, twenty-five Buddhas of whom Siddhartha Gautama was the last. In order to make sure that we do not confuse him with the other

Buddhas, we will henceforth, as far as possible, refer to him by name.

The Pali Canon does not offer us a complete or continuous account of the life of Gautama. The discourses are organized not chronologically, but according to their length or theme. Incidents from his life are scattered almost at random through the texts, and are mixed together with his teachings. There is almost no information about the early years of his life; the first major event that the texts relate in any detail is Gautama's departure from home at the age of twenty-nine to become a monk. We also have no way of knowing which of the anecdotes about his life are true, and which have been made up later by his followers. Many of the stories have a symbolic, rather than a literal meaning and supernatural beings, gods and demons play a major role in many of the incidents, so that it often becomes difficult to separate fact from myth.

Despite these difficulties, the Pali Canon does contain reliable information that has been possible to verify with other sources. For example, they mention Bimbisara, king of Magadha, and his son Ajatashatru; these were real people whose existence has been proven by historians and archaeologists.

The Pali Canon is also called the *Tipitaka*, or 'Three Baskets' because when the texts were written down they were divided into three sections. These are the *Sutta Pitaka*, i.e. the sermons given by Gautama, the *Vinaya Pitaka* or the rules of the Buddhist Order, and the *Abhidhamma Pitaka* which consists of philosophical discussions and analyses of Gautama's discourses. Only the first two sections contain information about Gautama's life.

Buddhism, like Hinduism, believes in reincarnation. Included in the *Sutta Pitaka* are the Jataka tales, some 550 stories and anecdotes that tell of the earlier incarnations of the Buddha. These tales were added between 300 BCE and 400 CE, several centuries after Gautama's death. They are interesting from the point of view of understanding the Buddhist vision of the Buddha. They also provide us with some biographical information about Gautama.

Since Pali was the language in which the Buddha's teachings were preserved and passed on, it also became the common language of the Buddhist monks all over India. Interestingly, Pali has no script of its own. When the Pali Canon was first written down in Sri Lanka, it was written down in the Sinhalese script. Wherever the Pali Canon has been written down, it has been done so in the script of that region or country. When it was transcribed in the West, it was done so in the Roman script.

The link between Pali and Sanskrit is quite evident. For example, consider the word *Nibbana* used in the Pali scriptures to describe the Buddha's freedom from the cycle of birth, death and rebirth; this is nothing but the Pali form of the more familiar Sanskrit word *Nirvana*. Or take the word *dhamma*, the Buddhist term for Gautama's teachings; the better known Sanskrit form is *dharma*. In the case of the Buddha's own name, we are more familiar with the Sanskrit 'Siddhartha Gautama', rather than the Pali 'Siddhattha Gotama'. In the Pali texts, the Buddha is referred to as 'Gotama', which was his clan name; his first name 'Siddhattha', is never used. Gautama, when referring to himself, calls himself 'Tathagata', the term used for an ascetic or monk. His followers also called him 'Bhagavat', or 'Lord'.

Pali was very closely related to the dialect known as Magadhi—the language the Buddha himself may have spoken, and the names as preserved in the Pali texts are probably as they were actually spoken in the Buddha's time. Therefore, while relating the story of the Buddha in the following chapters, we will refer to the Buddha as 'Siddhattha' or 'Gotama', i.e., using the Pali version of his names rather than the Sanskrit version; we shall do the same for names of the other people and places in his story. The glossary at the end lists all Pali names and terms as they appear in the book, and also gives their Sanskrit forms.

In the centuries after Gautama's death, Buddhists monks did attempt to write chronological and detailed accounts of his life. Two such accounts are the Sanskrit *Lalitavistara Sutra*, written in the third century CE, and the Pali *Nidana Katha*, written in the fifth century CE. both, however, deal only with the early life of Gautama; they are silent on the years he spent teaching and preaching his doctrine. They also glorify Gautama to the status of a divine being, and therefore give him superhuman powers and splatter his life with supernatural events. However, scholars believe that these texts are based on an ancient, but now lost, account of Gautama's life and therefore do contain some authentic material about Gautama's childhood and youth.

Hopelessly confusing though all this seems, and impossible though it may be to put together all the details of Gautama's life, the Buddhist scriptures do tell us about certain key events in his life: his birth, his renunciation of normal life, his enlightenment, the beginning of his life as a teacher, and his death. Stephen Batchelor, a Buddhist scholar, has attempted a chronological re-reading of the Pali Canon. He has reconstructed many details of the life of the Buddha, particularly of the forty-five years he spent teaching his doctrine to the world.

Let us bring together these various sources—the ancient Pali Canon, the Jataka tales, later biographies of Gautama, and the work of modern scholars such as Stephen Batchelor—and attempt our own reconstruction of the life of the Buddha.

Jataka
The Jataka tales, literally 'birth-stories', are fables and anecdotes depicting the previous incarnations—both animal and human—of the Buddha. These 547 tales, added to the Pali Canon several centuries after the Buddha's death, were used by monks and lay preachers to explain the Buddha's teachings. Some of these tales are very old and are found in the Vedas, which were composed more than a thousand years before the Buddha.

Others have been drawn from folklore, still others can be found in the Sanskrit *Panchatantram*, which was probably composed in the third century BCE.

With the spread of Buddhism, the stories spread around the world, to places like Indonesia, Thailand, Burma, Cambodia. In the second century BCE, Buddhist missionaries to Sri Lanka used these stories to spread the Buddha's word. In the sixth century CE they were translated into Persian upon the orders of the Persian king Khusro I. The Persian translation was later translated into Greek, Latin and Hebrew, and the tales found their way to Europe. Some of the tales are found in the ancient Greek collection of stories known as Aesop's fables. They also appear in later Indian collections, like the eleventh century *Katha Sarit Sagara* by Somadeva. We also find some of these tales in medieval European literature, for example, in the works of Chaucer in England and Boccaccio in Italy.

Many of the tales are set in or near Varanasi; according to the Pali Canon, the Buddha gave his first sermon at the nearby town of Sarnath. The Jatakas in the Pali Canon are all in verse, but it is probable that right from the beginning, these verses were accompanied by prose commentaries that were also passed on orally. These commentaries later evolved into the work known as the *Jatakatthakatha*.

The *Jatakatthakatha* contains all the verses of the Jataka, and gives in prose the stories connected with the verses. At the beginning of each story is given the circumstances in which the story was first told, and at the end, an identification of the main characters with the Buddha and his contemporaries. The work is in Pali, and is believed to have been composed by Buddhaghosa in the fifth century CE.

2 ⚚ Birth: 563 BCE

The exact year of his birth is still disputed. Though most scholars now accept that Siddhattha Gotama was born more than 2,500 years ago, most probably in the year 563 BCE, some say that he was born a century or more later. The Buddhist scriptures tell us that he was the son of Suddhodana, head of the warrior Sakya tribe, and his wife, Maha Maya. Maha Maya was the daughter of the chief of the Koliya clan, another people whose land adjoined that of the Sakyans. The Sakyans and the Koliyas believed that they were descended from a common ancestor. Though constantly at war with each other, they also regarded each other as kin, and intermarriage between them was common.

Since Gotama belonged to the Sakya tribe, he is also called 'Sakyamuni' or 'the sage of the Sakyans'. Within the Sakya tribe were several clans, or *gotta*. The Buddha belonged to the *Gotamagotta*—thus 'Gotama' was his clan name, and used much like a surname is today.

The land of the Sakyans lay in the north of India, across the foothills of the Himalayas. Though most Buddhist sources say that Suddhodana was a king, the ancient Pali scriptures show that he was really a provincial governor. The Sakyans followed the republican form of government, which means that their chief was an elected leader, not a hereditary king. The Sakyans were not an independent people; they were vassals of the powerful king of Kosala, who ruled over a kingdom that stretched from the northern bank of the Ganga river all the way up to the Himalayan foothills. The capital of the Sakyas was Kapilavatthu, a busy market town on the banks of the river Rohini. Though Gotama grew up in Kapilavatthu, he always called himself a Kosalan, and throughout his life remained loyal to the king of Kosala.

Buddhist scriptures give us the story of Gotama's birth in detail. It is said that one full moon night, as Maha Maya lay asleep, she had a strange and wonderful dream. She dreamt that she was carried away by the gods to a lake high up in the Himalayas. There she bathed, and was dressed by the gods in fine clothes and costly jewels. A white elephant, holding a white lotus in its trunk then appeared, and circling her three times, entered her womb from the right side. Next morning, she related the dream to her husband Suddhodana, who asked some wise men to explain it to him. The wise men, who were skilled at reading such signs, declared that Maha Maya's dream meant that she had conceived a son, who would either be a great king or a Buddha.

When the time for her delivery was close, Maha Maya asked her husband's permission to visit her parents, who lived in the nearby town of Devadaha. It was the custom then that a daughter should give birth in her parents' house. So Suddhodana agreed, and made arrangements for her journey. Maha Maya left for

Devadaha accompanied by attendants and soldiers to look after her. She had travelled only a few miles from Kapilavatthu when she passed the beautiful Lumbini garden. Tired, and wishing to rest for a while, Maha Maya ordered her attendants to stop. While wandering in the garden, she was overcome by labour pains, and almost immediately, she gave birth to a strong and lovely baby boy. It was the full moon day of the Indian calendar month of Vaisakh (which corresponds roughly to the modern month of April).

Mother and child were escorted back to Kapilavatthu at once, where Suddhodana received them with great joy. News of the baby's birth spread quickly amongst the people and celebrations broke out across the land.

The sage Asita, meditating in the Himalayas at the time, heard of the birth of Suddhodana's son and came at once to see him. Asita was a wise and learned man and had the ability to foretell the future. Suddhodana, pleased and honoured by the sage's visit, brought his baby son to him. 'Please tell me what my son's future will be,' he requested the sage, and placed the baby before him. The baby turned its tiny feet towards Asita who, surprised, examined the baby's feet carefully, and saw strange marks on them. Asita realized what the marks meant. 'This child will be a great teacher,' he said. Asita knew that he himself would not be alive to see the baby become a Buddha, and his eyes filled with tears of regret. Bowing his head and folding his hands, he paid reverence to the child. Suddhodana, seeing the sage salute his son, did the same.

When the baby was five days old, Suddhodana held the naming ceremony for his son. He invited one hundred and eight Brahmins to bless the baby and give him a name. Eight amongst the wise men invited had the ability to foretell the baby's future. Seven of them repeated the earlier prophecy that the child would be either a great king or a Buddha; but Kondanna, the eighth and the youngest of the Brahmins, said clearly that he would be a Buddha. Though the Pali scriptures do not say so explicitly, it can be inferred from other passages that the wise men named the child 'Siddhattha'.

Maha Maya did not live to see her son grow up. She died two days after his naming ceremony, when the baby was only seven days old. Siddhattha was nursed and brought up by Suddhodana's other wife, Pajapati. She was Maha Maya's younger sister and also married to Suddhodana.

Suddhodana did not want his son to become a Buddha for that would mean a life of hardship and poverty. How much better it would be, he thought, for his son to grow up to be a great and powerful king, the ruler of the world. He surrounded his son with every luxury possible; the child had nurses and attendants to look after him, and never knew a moment of want.

The Pali scriptures tell us very little about Siddhattha's early years. One of the few incidents from Siddhattha's childhood recorded in the Pali Canon describes a farming festival where Suddhodana himself joins the farmers in a ritual ploughing of the fields. Suddhodana takes his young son with him to the fields.

The child's attendants, distracted by the celebrations, leave him sitting alone under a rose-apple tree. When they return, they find him sitting cross-legged, deep in meditation; it is said that the shadow of the tree stayed still to protect him from the sun. The child's attendants bowed their heads before him in awe. Suddhodana, seeing his son deep in meditation was also overcome, and saluted him with folded hands. The scriptures relate this as Suddhodana's second salutation to his son.

The Pali scriptures are silent on Siddhattha's schooling. Chinese sources say that when he was eight years old, his father sent him to school. The Sanskrit *Lalitavistara Sutra* tells us that his teacher was called Viswamitra, and had been recommended as Siddhattha's tutor because he was learned in all forms of knowledge. Needless to say, all Buddhist accounts of Gotama's childhood say that Siddhattha was the best and the brightest in his class, that he surpassed all the other children in every field of learning. Children at the time were taught reading, writing, mathematics, languages, and sports such as wrestling and archery.

The Pali Canon contains no information about Siddhattha's teenage years; it says nothing about his education, or who his friends and companions were. We can conjecture that as his eldest son, Suddhodana would have involved Siddhattha in the daily tasks of governing the Sakyans. As chief of the Sakyans, Suddhodana would have made frequent visits to Savatthi, the capital of Kosala, and it is probable that he would have taken his son with him to train him early in the business of both politics and trade. Also, bearing in mind the prophecy regarding Siddhattha's future, and his father's desire that he become a king rather than an ascetic, it is more than likely that Suddhodana would have made sure that his son was not lost in the provincial obscurity of Kapilavatthu, but was known in the powerful and ambitious court circles of Savatthi. Perhaps this is where Siddhattha first met some of his future friends and companions, for instance, Pasenadi, the son of the king of Kosala.

Later accounts of Gotama's life mention his childhood rivalry with his cousin Devadatta, son of Suppabuddha, Siddhattha's maternal uncle. A well-known story relates how one day, Siddhattha and Devadatta decided to go for a walk in the woods. Though they were not planning to hunt, Devadatta carried his bow and arrows. Suddenly a swan appeared, flying overhead. Devadatta quickly fitted an arrow to his bow and shot the bird, which fell to the ground. Both boys ran towards it, but Siddhattha reached it first. He saw that the swan, though hurt, was still alive, and picked it up, cradling it gently in his arms. Devadatta declared that the bird was his since he had shot it, and demanded Siddhattha give it to him. But Siddhattha refused. 'Had the bird died, it would have been yours. But it is alive, and so it belongs to me,' he said. Devadatta did not agree, so Siddhattha suggested they take their quarrel to a wise old man who lived close by, and let him decide. The sage listened to both the boys and declared that a life belongs to the one who tries to save it, not to one who tries to destroy it. So, ruled the sage, the swan belonged to Siddhattha.

Devadatta's resentment of Gotama continued into their later years. The Pali Canon says that later he joined Gotama and became a monk in his Order. Even so, Devadatta could not shed his jealousy, and a few years before Gotama's death, plotted to kill Gotama and take over the Buddhist Order himself.

The Buddhist scholar, Stephen Batchelor, has put forward the theory that when Siddhattha was older, his father sent him to study at the University of Takkasila. Takkasila was the capital of Gandhara, a large and prosperous province that lay to the west of Kosala in what is now Pakistan. Gandhara was at that time part of the powerful Persian Empire, and Takkasila was home to one of the most renowned universities of the ancient world. The town lay at the junction of important trade routes, and travellers and merchants from all over the Persian Empire passed through it, giving it a vibrant, lively and cosmopolitan atmosphere. Young men from all over India were sent to study at Takkasila, where they were exposed to new ideas and new ways of thinking. Given that Siddhattha was from a respected and important family in the region, and his father's eldest son, it is very probable, says Batchelor, that he too was sent to study at Takkasila.

Batchelor supports this theory by his reading of Gotama's discourses as they are preserved in the Pali scriptures. In his sermons Gotama discusses concepts and ideas that are quite different from the traditional thinking prevalent in India at that time. Where, asks Batchelor, did Gotama learn to think differently? The logical answer, he believes, is at the University of Takkasila. Here Gotama would have met people from all parts of the known world, learnt about their civilizations, and been exposed to new ideas and philosophies. This exposure to fresh ideas in a multicultural atmosphere, says Batchelor, contributed to Gotama's distinctive thinking.

And, continues Batchelor, it was here, at the University, that he also met some of the men who would become his lifelong friends and companions.

Gotama's companions

Buddhist scriptures say that on the day of Gotama's birth were born several other beings, all of whom were to play an important part in Gotama's life. Some of these beings were:

The Bodhi tree under which Gotama attained enlightenment.

His future wife, and the one who was to be the mother of his son Rahula.

His elephant

His horse Kanthaka

His charioteer Channa

Kaludayi, the son of one of Suddhodana's ministers, and a childhood playmate of Gotama. He was called 'Udayi' because he was born on a day when the people were full of joy, and 'Kala' because of his dark skin. When Gotama left his home to become a monk, Suddhodana made Kaludayi one of his counsellors. Kaludayi soon became one of his most trusted men. After Gotama became a Buddha, Suddhodana sent several of his ministers to invite his son to Kapilavatthu. Each of the men he sent joined Gotama and forgot his mission to bring him back to Kapilavatthu. Only Kaludayi succeeded. He went to Gotama, and listening to his discourses, himself became a monk. He did not forget however the mission he had been entrusted with, and invited Gotama to spend the rainy season at Kapilavatthu. Gotama accepted the invitation, and was received with great joy and honour by his people.

Kosala

One of the four most powerful kingdoms in northern India during Gotama's life (the other three were Magadha, Vatsa and Avanti).

Location:
Corresponding to the Awadh region of the modern Indian state of Uttar Pradesh, it lay north of the Ganga, to the north-west of Magadha and next to Kasi, and extended across both banks of the Ghaghara River, and north into what is now Nepal.

Size: Approximately equal to the modern country of France

Capital: Savatthi
Other important cities: Saketa and Ayojjha

Important rulers:

Kingdom of the legendary King Rama of the Ramayana

In the Buddha's time:

Maha Kosala (?–538 BCE)

Abdicated in favour of his son Pasenadi (c. 538–484 BCE)

The Buddha's friend, patron and benefactor

Overthrown by his son, Vidudabha (c. 484–482 BCE)

His only achievement seems to be the slaughter and annihilation of the Sakya tribe.

After Vidudabha's death, Kosala was taken over and annexed by the kingdom of Magadha.

Subject territories:

Kasi (the land around modern Varanasi)

The land of the Sakyans, with its capital at Kapilavatthu.

3 ✦ Friends

Gotama inspired loyalty and deep affection in the people who knew him. Many of the friends and companions of his younger days remained with him till the end of his life. Five men in particular are mentioned in the Pali scriptures—Pasenadi, king of Kosala; Bandhula, his commander in chief; Mahali, a Licchavi nobleman; Jivaka, physician to the king of Magadha, and also Gotama's doctor; and Angulimala, the son of a priest and a serial murderer. All five men were Gotama's contemporaries and about the same age as him. They had all been educated at the University of Takkasila, and knew each other well. If, as Stephen Batchelor suggests and is very likely, Gotama too had been educated at Takkasila, he would have known these men since the age of sixteen or seventeen if not earlier. Gotama had a deep and unique bond with each of them; all held Gotama in great respect and became a follower of his teachings as a Buddha, though only Angulimala actually became a monk. Their lives were entwined with Gotama's, and they appear again later in his story. So let us pause awhile and become better acquainted with them.

Pasenadi

He was one of Gotama's closest friends, and later, as king of Kosala, also his chief patron and benefactor. It is probable that Gotama, as the son of an important chieftain of the region, knew Pasenadi, the young prince of Kosala, even before the boys were old enough to be sent away to Takkasila. After Gotama became a Buddha, Pasenadi's favour and friendship became critical to his mission. Without the king's support, Gotama would not have been able to teach in Savatthi, nor gather the support that he did in Kosala. Of all the friends of his youth, Gotama's life was most closely linked with that of Pasenadi. The political, and even personal, ups and downs in Pasenadi's life directly affected Gotama and his work as a Buddha.

Pasenadi was the son of Maha Kosala, the king of Kosala. Pasenadi himself became the king of Kosala while still a young man. When, after completing his education at Takkasila, he returned home to Savatthi, his father was so pleased with his ability and his accomplishments, that he made him king at once. Pasenadi was a good king. He worked hard to improve the administration of his country, and tried, unsuccessfully, to stamp out corruption amongst his ministers. He enjoyed the company of learned men, and encouraged them with gifts of land and gold.

Pasenadi was very friendly with Bimbisara, the king of Magadha. Magadha lay to the south of the Ganga, while Kosala lay to the north. It was a kingdom far more powerful than Kosala. It was also richer: Bimbisara had five millionaires in his kingdom, while Pasenadi had none. Pasenadi asked Bimbisara to let one of them move to Kosala, so that Kosala too could benefit from his wealth. Bimbisara gave him Dhananjaya, son of Mendaka, one of the rich men. Pasenadi married one of Bimbisara's sisters, probably as part of a diplomatic alliance; his own sister Kosaladevi was married to Bimbisara, perhaps as part of the same alliance.

Some sources say that Suddhodana and Bimbisara's father were friends and that Gotama and Bimbisara had been childhood playmates. After attaining enlightenment, Gotama spent a great deal of time in Rajagaha, Bimbisara's capital city. Bimbisara became a follower of his teachings, and treated him with unfailing respect and courtesy, and even gave him land in Rajagaha where he could set up his community. Bimbisara was five years younger than Gotama; he died eight years before Gotama did. Bimbisara's death was a tragic one—he was imprisoned, then starved and tortured by his son Ajatasattu. We shall see later how the lives of these three men—Pasenadi, Bimbisara and Gotama—came together at the point of Bimbisara's death.

Pasenadi became a follower of Gotama very early on—the Tibetan scriptures say that it was in the second year after Gotama became a Buddha. He extended his royal support and protection not only to Gotama but also to his followers, and was quick to honour those who honoured Gotama. At the same time, Pasenadi was a tolerant king and respected men of all religions. It is said that the alms hall in the royal palace was always open, providing food and drink to the hungry.

Pasenadi visited Gotama as often as he could, sometimes three times a day. The two men talked to each other as equals; Pasenadi did not hesitate to discuss even his most personal matters with Gotama. Pasenadi's favourite wife was Mallika, a garland maker's daughter. The king, captivated by her beauty and intelligence, and perhaps influenced by Gotama's ideas, had disregarded her low caste and married her. Mallika too, was a follower of Gotama's teachings. When Mallika gave birth to a daughter, a frustrated and angry Pasenadi confided to Gotama how disappointed he was that his most beloved wife had not given him a son. But Gotama pointed out to him the virtues of daughters, and Pasenadi realized his foolishness. He came to love his daughter dearly. He named her Vajira; she was his only daughter.

Pasenadi loved his food—he was a large eater, and it is said that the bowl he ate out of was the size of a cartwheel. Not surprisingly, he was also overweight! Gotama advised him to eat less, and gave him a sermon on the benefits of moderation. So that Pasenadi would not forget, Gotama taught his nephew a poem on the advantages of self control which he told the boy to recite every time his uncle sat down to eat! Pasenadi, not allowed to forget, gave up his large meals and soon became slim and healthy.

One of Pasenadi's sisters, Sumana, joined Gotama and became a nun.

Pasenadi wanted his relationship with Gotama to become even closer and stronger. He therefore decided to link himself to the Buddha's family, by marrying one of Gotama's many cousins. The Sakyans, though vassals to the king of Kosala, were a haughty people. They decided it was beneath them to give one of their daughters in marriage to Pasenadi. At the same time, they did not want to anger him by refusing outright. So they sent him the daughter of a slave woman as his bride. The girl was called Vasabha. Though Vasabha's father was Gotama's own cousin Mahanama (the son of Amitodana, Suddhodana's brother), she was not a noblewoman because her mother was a slave. Sending her as a bride to the king was not just disrespectful of the Sakyans, but also unwise. Pasenadi, assuming Vasabha to be of noble birth, married her; he found out about the fraud years later, and only Gotama could calm his anger. This foolish act of the Sakyans had consequences far beyond what they could have imagined. We will see later its impact not only on Pasenadi, but also on the Sakyans themselves, and of course, on Gotama.

Pasenadi remained Gotama's close friend and follower till the end.

Bandhula

Bandhula was the son of a chieftain of the Malla tribe. The land of the Mallas lay south of the Sakyan province. Like the Sakyans, the Mallas too had a republican form of government. The important members of the tribe administered the land in turn; those who were not busy with government engaged in trade, often making long caravan journeys for the purpose. Their capital (and Bandhula's home) was Kusinara, a small insignificant town, which Ananda, one of Gotama's disciples, scornfully described as a 'branch township, with wattle-and-daub houses in the midst of the jungle'. This was also the place where Gotama died.

Bandhula too had been a student at Takkasila and was close to both Gotama and Pasenadi. After finishing at Takkasila, Bandhula returned home to Kusinara. But disgusted with the jealousy and pettiness of the other noble families of Malla, he decided to move to Savatthi where his friend Pasenadi had become king. Pasenadi made Bandhula his *senapati*, the commander of his army.

Bandhula's wife was also called Mallika. Both Bandhula and Mallika held Gotama in great reverence. When Mallika failed to have babies, Bandhula decided to send her back to her parents. Before she left, Mallika went to say farewell to Gotama; he told her to return to her husband. Bandhula accepted her back because of his great faith in Gotama. Soon after, Mallika gave birth to twin sons. Legend says that Mallika bore Bandhula thirty-two sons, giving birth to twin sons sixteen times!

Bandhula was also known for his wisdom; one day he retried a case where the appointed judge had given an incorrect decision. Pasenadi, impressed by his judgement, appointed him chief justice. But the other judges, jealous of Bandhula, poisoned the king's mind against him.

Influenced by his corrupt counsellors, Pasenadi sent Bandhula and his sons to put down a rebellion on the borders of Kosala and ordered that they be killed on their way back.

Mallika heard the news of the death of her husband and her sons when she was serving food to five hundred Buddhist monks whom she had invited. Some say that Gotama himself was present at the meal. She remained calm till all the monks had eaten. She then called her daughters-in-law and told them what had happened. She asked them to stay calm, and hold no anger against Pasenadi for, she said, the king would himself repent the killing of his old friend. She was right, and soon Pasenadi, overcome by grief and remorse, begged her forgiveness. 'Ask any boon of me,' he said. Mallika asked that she and her thirty-two daughters-in-law be allowed to return home to Kusinara in peace. Pasenadi did not go unpunished for Bandhula's murder; it was avenged by Bandhula's nephew Dighakaranya, many years later.

After Bandhula's death, Mallika gave up wearing jewellery and fine clothes, and lived quietly and simply in Kusinara. She had one rare and valuable possession: a jewelled cloak of rare beauty, which she put away. She never forgot Gotama and revered him throughout her life. When she heard that Gotama had breathed his last in Kusinara, the very city in which she lived, she went to pay him her last respects. She took with her the jewelled cloak, which she had washed in perfumed water. As they carried Gotama's body away for cremation, Mallika placed her cloak on the Buddha's bier. She asked only that in each of her future births she be given a body that would need no jewels, but which would appear as though it always bore them.

Mahali

Mahali belonged to the rich and powerful Licchavi tribe, whose capital was the city of Vesali in Vajji. He was close to Bandhula and Pasenadi as well. After Takkasila, Mahali returned to Vesali, and gave himself to educating the young men of his tribe. Sadly, he lost his sight when still a young man. Though blind, he continued to teach, and for his efforts was given a house by the city gate which led to Savatthi from Vesali. He was also given the revenue from this gate as income.

Mahali was also a favourite of Bimbisara. When the people of Vesali wanted to invite Gotama as the Buddha to their city, Mahali was sent as one of their two representatives to Bimbisara to ask him to persuade Gotama to visit them.

Jivaka

Jivaka was the most famous doctor of his day. His full name was Jivaka Komarabhacca. His mother was Salavati, a courtesan who lived in Rajagaha, the capital of Magadha. As soon as he was born, Salavati placed her son in a basket and threw him onto a rubbish heap. One of Bimbisara's sons, Abhayarajakumar, was passing by, and noticed the baby in the basket. When the prince asked about the child, people replied that 'he was alive' (*jivati*)—and so the baby was named 'Jivaka'. Prince Abhaya took pity on the child, and ordered that he be taken to the palace and brought up as his own son. Since he was brought up by the prince (*rajakumara*), he was called 'Komarabhacca'. Some scholars say that 'Komarabhacca' means someone who was skilled in treating children, and that his name refers to his skill and not to the prince who adopted him.

When Jivaka grew up, he found out the story of his birth. Disillusioned, he decided to leave Rajagaha without telling the prince, his foster father. He went to Takkasila, where he studied medicine for seven years. When he had learnt all that he could, his teacher gave him some money and sent him away, declaring him qualified to practise medicine. Jivaka ultimately returned to Rajagaha, where Prince Abhaya set him up in his own house. Soon his talent as a doctor and a surgeon became known, and he was called upon to treat the king, Bimbisara, himself. Bimbisara, pleased with Jivaka's cure, appointed him royal physician; he was also appointed physician to Gotama and his monks who were living in Rajagaha at the time.

Jivaka was called upon to attend the rich and the famous of Magadha. But of all the people he looked after, Jivaka's greatest joy lay in looking after Gotama. He helped Gotama on many occasions. Once, Devadatta hurled a rock at Gotama in a clumsy attempt to kill him; Gotama hurt his foot and had to be carried to Jivaka's house, where Jivaka treated and bandaged the injured foot. He soon became a follower of Gotama's teachings. He became so attached to Gotama that he built a monastery for him in a mango grove upon his own estate in Rajagaha. It is said that as far as possible, Jivaka visited Gotama three times a day.

After Bimbisara's death, Jivaka continued to serve Ajatasattu; it was Jivaka who brought Ajatasattu to Gotama after the murder of Bimbisara. Ajatasattu became an ardent follower of Gotama, and hosted the First Buddhist Council to preserve Gotama's teachings.

Jivaka, despite being a very busy man, never slipped in his attention to Gotama or his monks. Many people who could not afford to pay for Jivaka's services became monks under Gotama so that they could get free treatment. When Jivaka found out how people were taking advantage of Gotama, he asked Gotama to make a rule that men suffering from certain diseases should not be allowed to become monks. He also recommended that Gotama order his monks to take exercise—he had gone to Vesali on business and had noticed how unhealthy some of them looked!

Angulimala

Angulimala was Gotama's only friend from Takkasila who also became a monk. His story is also perhaps the saddest.

He was the son of Bhaggava, a priest at the court of the king of Kosala. It is said that the night Angulimala was born, all the armour in the town of Savatthi shone brightly. But since no one was harmed, the baby was named Ahimsaka, which means 'the non-violent one'.

At Takkasila, he was a favourite of his teacher's, but his fellow students grew jealous, and turned the teacher against him. When Angulimala finished his education, and the time came for him to leave, the teacher demanded his honorarium—a thousand human right-hand fingers. Ahimsaka had no choice but to give in to his teacher's demand.

He returned to Kosala, and hid himself in a dense forest. He began to waylay travellers and kill them, taking a right-hand finger from each person that he killed. He strung the fingers into a garland, which he wore round his neck; he was thus given the name 'Angulimala' from *anguli* which means 'finger' and *mala* which means 'garland' or 'necklace'.

The people who lived near the forest were terrified of Angulimala. They left their homes and villages and ran away as far as they could. No one had any idea who he was, or why he killed the way he did. Pasenadi, who was king of Kosala now, concerned for the safety of his people, sent a detachment of soldiers to hunt down the bandit and kill him.

Angulimala's mother, Mantani, was the only one who suspected the truth—she had guessed that the fearsome bandit was none other than her son Ahimsaka. Learning of the king's orders, she set off for the forest to warn her son. By then Angulimala had already killed 999 people. He needed one more to complete his thousand. As he lay hidden amongst the trees, waiting for his thousandth victim, he saw his mother enter the forest. Tired of living in the forest and impatient to fulfil his teacher's demand, Angulimala decided he could not spare his mother.

Meanwhile, Gotama too had heard of Angulimala and of Pasenadi's orders to kill him, and he too had set off for the forest. He reached there just in time. As Angulimala got ready to ambush his mother and kill her, Gotama stepped in front of him. Angulimala, relieved that he did not have to kill his mother after all, prepared to kill Gotama. But Gotama spoke to him, and hearing his words, Angulimala put down the sword and gave up his murdering ways.

Gotama took Angulimala back to his monastery with him, where Angulimala became a monk.

Meanwhile Pasenadi, the king, was still in search of the bandit. Unable to find him, he went to see Gotama and ask his advice. Gotama brought Angulimala before him. The man who had been a serial murderer was now a monk, dressed in yellow robes, his head shaven. Pasenadi was overcome with wonder, and acknowledging Angulimala's great metamorphosis, offered to look after all his needs. But Angulimala remained steady in his vows and refused his offer.

According to the Pali scriptures, this happened in the twentieth year after Gotama attained enlightenment.

When Angulimala went to Savatthi to beg for alms, the people shouted abuse at him and pelted him with stones. Gotama told him to bear their attacks as punishment for the murders he had committed.

Angulimala died very soon after he became a monk.

Such were some of Gotama's friends—men and women whose lives touched Gotama's, who were inspired by him and deeply influenced by his teachings. Gotama's friends were vital, vibrant people with real concerns and human passions, and Gotama too was a man before he was a saint. One of Gotama's greatest qualities was his ability to understand and empathize with the human condition. He was a man very much of his times. He was not a recluse or a wandering ascetic as we sometimes imagine him to be. Despite having renounced the world, he was in touch with it, and directly affecting and affected by people and events.

Before we can truly understand his interaction with the world as a Buddha, we need to understand, if we can, why he chose the life he did. As Suddhodana's son, he had available to him luxury, power and learning. So why did he give up his comfortable existence as a nobleman and choose the life of a monk?

A cloak beyond compare

The jewelled cloak that Mallika, Bandhula's wife, placed upon Gotama's bier, was made of gold and precious jewels, and so costly and rare that only three such cloaks existed. The first was owned by Mallika herself, the second by the daughter of the treasurer of the kingdom of Kasi, and the third by Visakha, Gotama's most important female lay disciple.

Visakha was the daughter of Dhananjaya, the millionaire's son from Magadha whom Bimbisara had given leave to settle in Kosala.

Buddhist sources give a detailed description of Visakha's cloak. It was fashioned by five hundred goldsmiths working day and night for four months. In its making were used four pots of diamonds, eleven pots of pearls, twenty-two of coral, thirty-three pots of rubies, and gold and silver beyond measure. Woven into the fabric of the cloak was a peacock with five hundred golden feathers in each wing, a beak made of coral, and jewels for eyes, the neck feathers and the tail. As the wearer of this moved, the feathers moved musically.

The cloak was so heavy, that only a woman who had the strength of five elephants could carry it. Visakha was strong enough to wear it.

Magadha

In Gotama's time, the most powerful state in northern India.

Location:

It lay south of the Ganga, in territory corresponding roughly to the modern Indian state of Bihar. At the time of the Buddha, the kingdom of Magadha was bounded on the east by the river Champa, which flowed between Magadha and Anga, on the south by the Vindhya mountains, on the west by the river Sona, and on the north by the river Ganga.

Capital: Rajagaha (modern Rajgir)

Other important cities: Pataliputta, which grew from a small village in the Buddha's time to an important port city on the banks of the Ganga. Later, it replaced Rajagaha as the capital of Magadha.

Magadha's location along the Ganga valley enabled it to control both trade and communication along the river. The river also gave it access to the rich ports in the Ganga delta.

The Buddha's chief disciples, Sariputta and Moggallana, came from Magadha.

Important rulers:

Bimbisara (c. 542–491 BCE)

At the age of sixty-seven abdicated in favour of his son, Ajatasattu, who imprisoned him and starved him to death

Ajatasattu (c. 491–461 BCE)

Two centuries later, the Mauryan emperor Ashoka (c. 269–232 BCE)

Subject territories:

Anga, a small kingdom on the borders of modern Bengal; annexed by Bimbisara

Kasi; though under Kosalan rule, Bimbisara received part of Kasi as the dowry of his queen Kosaladevi, the sister of King Pasenadi of Kosala

Kosala, annexed by Ajatasattu soon after the death of Vidudabha, Pasenadi's successor

Vajji, annexed by Ajatasattu after a long-drawn-out war

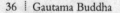

4 ❀ Renunciation: 534 BCE

When Siddhattha had completed his education Suddhodana decided to get him married. The Pali scriptures do not tell us very much about the circumstances of his wedding. Later texts, though, describe the event in some detail.

Suddhodana had not forgotten the prophecy made at Siddhattha's birth that he would either grow up to become a Buddha or a great king. He did not want his son to give up the world and become an ascetic. So when his son was old enough, the wise men and women of his tribe advised him to get the boy married. Once married, they said, he would learn the pleasures of life and not be tempted to retire from the world.

Suddhodana agreed and sent messengers to all the Sakyans, asking them to allow Siddhattha to choose one of their daughters as a wife. The Sakyans refused. The young man, they said, was handsome, but did he have the ability to support a wife? What skills did he possess? What learning did he have? When Siddhattha heard this, he called the Sakyans together and demonstrated to them his ability in various arts including calligraphy and arithmetic, his skill in running, leaping, wrestling and other sports. The Sakyans, reassured that Siddhattha would indeed make a good husband, sent their daughters to him. From amongst all the young girls who came forward to be his wife, Siddhattha chose Bimba, or Bimbasundari, the daughter of his maternal uncle Suppabuddha, and the sister of Devadatta. (Some texts however say that she was the daughter of Dandapani, the brother of Suppabuddha). She was a learned and independent-minded woman, a good match in every way for the talented young Siddhattha.

In later texts Bimba is known by other names—Gopa, Yashodhara, Subhaddaka and Bhaddakacca. It is possible that some of these names were adjectives to describe her, and which later came to be used as proper names. For instance, 'Bhaddakacca' means 'the woman whose body is like burnished gold'. This name indicates her great beauty. In the Buddhist texts, she is most commonly referred to as 'Rahulamata', or the mother of Gotama's son, Rahula.

Bimba had been born on the same day as Gotama. Tibetan sources say that Bimba and Gotama were married to each other at the age of sixteen, while Chinese sources say that they were nineteen. Their son Rahula was born when they were both twenty-nine years old. This was rather late by the standards of their times, when men and women were married in their teens and had children right away. Stephen Batchelor suggests they could have been married later than the texts state, a possibility if Gotama had been away at Takkasila.

Gotama lived a life of ease for many years. Suddhodana made sure his son had every material comfort he could desire. It is said that Gotama owned three palaces, one for each of the three seasons—summer, winter and the rains. There was nothing that Gotama did not have, and there seemed no reason why he should ever give up his luxurious life as a Sakyan nobleman. And yet, at the age of twenty-nine, when his newborn son was only a day old, Gotama walked away from his palace in Kapilavatthu to become a monk. Why did he do so?

In answer, the *Nidana Katha* gives us the story of the Four Signs. Suddhodana, mindful of the prophecy made at Siddhattha's birth, had made sure that his son should see no sign of human suffering. But destiny cannot be denied, and one day there arose in Siddhattha a desire to ride out beyond the palace walls. As he rode out in his chariot with his charioteer Channa, he saw before him an old man. The man was bent with age, his hair was white, his eyes were dim, his skin lined and wrinkled, and his limbs shrunken and trembling so that he could barely walk. Siddhattha was horrified; he had never seen anyone like this before. He asked Channa what had happened to the man, and Channa explained that he had simply grown old.

Siddhattha returned home, his heart filled with despair. When Suddhodana heard of the incident, he surrounded his son with pleasures of all kinds to make him forget. A few days later, Siddhattha rode out again. This time he saw a sick man, and once again returned home filled with grief. The next time he rode out beyond the palace walls, he saw a corpse being carried on a bier to the cremation grounds and came home troubled and distressed. He realized that pain and suffering were inevitable in every human life. Finally, on a fourth occasion, Siddhattha rode past a man dressed in yellow robes. The man's head was shaven, and he carried a begging bowl in his hand; but he looked happy and at peace. When Siddhattha asked Channa who he was, Channa explained that he was an ascetic who had given up the worldly life. Siddhattha's heart filled with happiness and he fell into deep thought. Some sources say that Siddhattha saw the Four Signs—the old man, the sick man, the corpse and the ascetic—all on the same day.

On his way home, Siddhattha received the news that his wife had given birth to a son; he decided to call his son 'Rahula' which means 'bond'. As he rode by in his chariot, Kisagotami, a young noblewoman, saw him from her balcony. She was enchanted by his handsome looks, and filled with love for him, sang aloud a song which contained the word *nibbuta*, which means 'at peace'. Siddhattha was touched by the significance of the word—his own thoughts had been with the ascetic and his look of peaceful happiness. In gratitude, he sent Kisagotami the necklace that he was wearing. He reached home in a very thoughtful mood.

That night, at the palace, Siddhattha woke suddenly to find that the musicians and dancers who had been entertaining him earlier in the evening had fallen asleep around his couch. In sleep they had lost all their beauty and grace—some slept with their mouths open, some were snoring, and each and every one of those beautiful women looked ugly and repulsive. Disgusted with the sight, and his heart full of the suffering that he had seen in the old man, the sick man and the corpse, Siddhattha decided there and then to leave the worldly life.

He called Channa his charioteer, and asked him to saddle his horse Kanthaka. He went to his wife's room for a last look at her and their newborn son. He did not want to wake her because he knew that if he spoke to her he would not be able to leave; he gazed at her silently, then turning, tiptoed away. Some versions of the story say that Siddhattha left seven days after the birth of his son. This important event in Siddhattha Gotama's life is known as the Renunciation.

Gotama left Kapilavatthu on his horse Kanthaka; Channa followed him, clinging to the horse's tail, begging him not to leave. As Gotama passed the gates of the city, he was overcome by doubt—what if he stayed behind and became instead a great ruler, as his father wanted him to be? Wouldn't that be easier? He could end the world's suffering through his wise governance. Was it really necessary to give up everything he knew, and leave behind all the people he loved? But Gotama shrugged off his fears and continued on his way. Outside the city, he stopped and turned his horse around for one last long look at the city of his childhood and youth. Then, with Channa still following him faithfully, he rode through the lands of the Sakyans, the Koliyas and the Mallas till he reached the river Anoma. Kanthaka crossed the river in a single powerful leap. On the other side, Gotama took off his ornaments and fine clothes, and put on the yellow robe of the ascetic; taking up his sword, he cut off his hair and beard. He then asked Channa to return to Kapilavatthu with Kanthaka. But the horse refused to leave his master, and broken-hearted, died there beside the Anoma river.

This version of Gotama's renunciation is taken from the *Nidana Katha*. Passages in the Pali scriptures show that his decision to leave the world was a gradual process, and not brought about by any dramatic events. Though in the Pali texts Gotama himself refers to the Four Signs, he talks about them as events not in his own life, but in the life of Vipassi, another Buddha who had lived several centuries before him. The story of the Four Signs leading up to the renunciation is not meant to be taken as historical truth. It is a mythological tale, which symbolizes Gotama's acceptance of suffering as a reality of human existence, and his realization that denying it, or closing his eyes to it, would not make it go away.

The Pali texts record Gotama's own explanation for his decision to leave home. He gave up the worldly life, he said, to search for freedom from the bondage of birth, death and rebirth which led only to death again. He was troubled by questions of life and death: Why am I alive? What is the meaning of this life? Why are we born, only to die again? All that he had done and learnt seemed meaningless. So he decided to seek a new way, by giving up all that was familiar and comfortable and beloved. It could not have been an easy decision for him. It would have needed tremendous courage and determination for him to actually go through with it. It also caused great grief to those who loved him. His parents begged him to stay back, and wept to see their son leave his comfortable home to become a wandering monk. His wife gave up all luxuries, and lived as he would have lived, dressed in yellow robes and eating only one meal a day.

The path he had chosen to tread would not be easy. It would be full of struggle and doubt and uncertainty. He did not know what lay ahead of him, and whether he would ever reach the truth that he was seeking. But Gotama was not to be deflected from his purpose— there must be a way to rise above suffering, and he was determined to find it.

Mara

Buddhist books contain many stories of a being called Mara. This was not a real person, but a mythological figure, the personification of Death. He is also the Evil One, the Tempter who tries to distract Gotama and his monks from following the path to Enlightenment.

The later books, especially the *Nidana Katha*, describe the many encounters that Gotama has with Mara. One such encounter occurs on the night of his Renunciation: as he leaves Kapilavatthu, Mara stops him and urges him to return home, promising him that he would become a great king in a week's time. Of course, Gotama does not listen to Mara and continues on his way. Mara appears again when Gotama is on the verge of attaining enlightenment. The stories describe how

Mara gathers a huge army and prepares to attack Gotama, who is sitting in meditation. Once again Gotama vanquishes Mara.

Mara is therefore nothing but the doubts and fears that assailed Gotama and his monks as they struggled to reach the Truth. He represents the irritations and inconveniences, the distractions and worldly temptations that appeared to lead them astray.

Mara has the ability to change his form, and appears in various shapes and guises in the stories. Once, while Gotama was preaching to the monks, Mara arrived in the form of a bullock and broke their earthenware bowls which had been set out to dry. At another time he came as a peasant who interrupted Gotama's discourse to ask if anyone had seen his oxen. A third time he entered into the householders of a city where Gotama and his monks had gone to beg for food; none of the householders gave them anything and the monks returned with empty bowls. Mara whispered to Gotama to go back and try again, but Gotama refused saying he preferred to remain hungry that day.

In Pali literature, Mara has many names. He is called 'Namuci', the one whom none can escape, and 'Vasavatti', the one who rules all. The stories around Mara are very complex and it is not always easy to understand their meaning.

After leaving home, Gotama walked for many days, till he crossed the Ganga and reached the city of Rajagaha, modern Rajgir, the capital of the powerful kingdom of Magadha. In Gotama's day, Rajagaha was one of the most prosperous and heavily populated cities of the world. High mountains encircled the city protectively while tall stone walls provided further defence against enemy attack. Rajagaha was a major commercial centre, and a constant stream of merchants, traders and travellers flowed in and out of its gates. It was also an industrial centre, with copper and iron mines close by. Natural springs provided a regular supply of water, and parks and gardens graced the city. It was a favourite gathering place of monks and ascetics, who could always be sure of a welcome from the citizens of Rajagaha, and from their king Bimbisara.

As we saw earlier, some versions of the Buddhist scriptures say that Gotama and Bimbisara had been childhood friends. But, according to the oldest part of the Pali Canon, Gotama and Bimbisara met only after Gotama's renunciation. As Gotama walked through the streets of Rajagaha begging for alms, Bimbisara saw him from the roof of his palace. Taken by the young monk's noble appearance, the king sent his men to find out who he was and where he was staying. The king's men followed Gotama to the foot of the hill known as Pandava Pabbata, where Gotama sat down to eat his meal and rest. The men rushed back to the king, who, mounting his chariot, came at once to meet the monk. He was so impressed by Gotama that he offered to make him his heir. Gotama refused, explaining to the king that he had left the worldly life and was in search of the path that would take him beyond human suffering. Bimbisara accepted his refusal, but made him promise that once he had found the answers he sought, the first city he would visit would be Rajagaha.

It is not important which version of the story is historically true; what is of greater significance is the fact that Gotama, as the son of an important nobleman of Kosala, was comfortable interacting with kings and aristocrats. Pasenadi, king of Kosala, was his contemporary and most likely a friend from his youth; Bimbisara, the most powerful monarch of the region, perhaps knew him since childhood, or if not, knew his father as chief of the Sakyas. Though Gotama never introduced himself as the son of Suddhodana, it cannot be denied that later, after he became a Buddha and set out to establish an order of monks to spread his teachings, the friendships of his youth stood him in good stead. Many of the men who had known him as Suddhodana's son came to listen to him preach, and became his followers. Many of them were both wealthy and influential and they helped Gotama in different ways—they set up monasteries, made sure that his monks had food, clothing and medical aid, and were free from inconvenience and discomfort. Most importantly, their support and protection made it possible for Gotama and his monks to move about freely and safely from land to land, spreading his word. The people, seeing their king or chieftain treat Gotama with reverence, also paid him the same respect. These factors are important in explaining the rapid spread of Gotama's teachings, both during his lifetime and after his death.

The Pali scriptures relate that Gotama did not stay long in Rajagaha this time, but continued on his travels in search of the path that would help him overcome suffering. From Rajagaha he journeyed to Vesali in the republic of Vajji; Vesali was the capital city of the Licchavi tribe. Here he became a disciple of a teacher called Alara Kalama. Alara's philosophy was based on the idea that ignorance, not desire, was the cause of human suffering. He believed that the only way to end suffering was to rise above this transient world by uniting with *Brahman*, the Absolute Spirit. He said that this could be achieved through intense meditation on 'nothingness'. Gotama quickly mastered Alara's teachings, and soon surpassed him, but did not find in his methods an end to suffering. He left Alara and joined another teacher, Uddaka Ramaputta; but Uddaka's teachings also did not give him the answers he sought, and very soon he left Uddaka as well.

After leaving Alara and Uddaka, Gotama went to a place called Uruvela, which is today the busy, bustling town of Bodh Gaya. In Gotama's time, Uruvela was a small settlement on the banks of the Neranjara river. Here Gotama met other monks like himself, many of whom were on quests similar to his own. The Buddhist texts mention five men in particular—these were the five Brahmins Kondanna, Bhaddiya, Vappa, Mahanama and Assaji. Kondanna was the youngest of the eight Brahmins who had foretold Gotama's future at his naming ceremony; the other four were the sons of four of the other Brahmins who had been present that day. They had been told by their fathers of the prophecy made at Gotama's birth, and to join him should he renounce the world. They therefore joined him at Uruvela as his friends and close companions. These five men are known in the texts as the Panchavaggiya monks. With their support, Gotama experimented with the most severe austerities—perhaps penance, he thought, would show him the way to overcome suffering.

Later, he described the tortures to which he subjected himself. He barely ate, he said, so that he became so thin that his bones stuck out. His arms and legs became like sticks of bamboo, his eyes sunk deep into his skull, his belly stuck to his backbone, his skin wrinkled and shrivelled up, and the hair on his body rotted at the roots and fell out. For six long years he abused his body, desperately searching for answers to his questions. But he found neither peace nor wisdom.

Gotama was not willing to give up. There must be another way, he said to himself. He then remembered the incident from his childhood when, taken to the farming festival by his father, he had been left alone under a rose-apple tree. He remembered how he had fallen into a meditative trance, and the feeling of extreme joy that he had experienced. Perhaps that could be the way to rise above suffering, he thought. For six years he had punished himself, denying every comfort, every pleasure. He had fought against desire in an effort to end suffering, but he had not succeeded. Yet, as a child, he had reached a state of joy without any effort at all. So, reasoned Gotama, could it be that it was possible that there was a less extreme way, a middle way, that avoided both the extremes of asceticism and the excesses of a life of self-indulgence? Gotama decided to find out.

Gotama knew he could not achieve any state of bliss while his body continued to suffer. He decided to go back to eating normal food, and ate some *kummasa*, a dish made of rice and thickened milk. His friends, the Panchavaggiya monks, thought he had given up; disappointed and losing all faith in him and the prophecy, they left him and went away to Isipatana (modern Sarnath) near Varanasi.

Gotama, of course, had not given up his search at all. He continued to live at Uruvela, slowly nursing his body back to health. He realized that before he could aspire to any state of bliss, he needed to understand his own human nature. He spent his days perfecting the practice of what he later called *sati* or 'mindfulness', which, he explained, meant becoming completely aware of what was happening in his own body, as well as in the world around him. Gotama became aware of how he walked, sat, stood, ate, drank, and even breathed; he became aware of every thought that passed through his mind, and every feeling that arose in him. He became convinced that the answers he sought lay within himself. Only by understanding his own nature, and by training his mind to be free of greed, desire and egotism, could he rise above suffering.

The practice of mindfulness also made Gotama realize more clearly the nature of suffering—it was not just old age, sickness and death; even the little daily disappointments and frustrations of life made up suffering. He also realized that the cause of this suffering was craving or desire—want or desire led to greed, anger, envy, fear and hatred. All this was suffering. Human beings were in a state of constant wanting, and the world, by its very nature, was shifting and transient. Gotama realized that to live in the world with any possibility of happiness, it was necessary to stop worrying about what had happened in the past or what may happen in the future. It was important, instead, to focus on the present; the present, said Gotama, was the fruit of the past, and the seed of the future. Only by being mindful of the present, he said, could one hope to engage with the world with detachment, compassion and clarity.

Gotama did not stop at mindfulness. He also trained his mind to become free of the thoughts and emotions that led to suffering. He did this through intense yogic exercises and meditation. Each day he would sit in meditation and empty his mind of the thoughts that led to anger, anxiety, uncertainty, hatred, greed or laziness.

His aim was to free himself completely from egotism, so that he had no personal wants or desires, and could look upon the world with compassion and kindness. This state of compassion, if taken to very high levels, would free the mind, make it limitless and able to embrace all creation without hatred or anger. This 'release of the mind' was the awakening, the enlightenment, which Gotama sought.

Buddhist scriptures say that Gotama attained supreme enlightenment in a single night. This, of course cannot be true—the process would have been a long and difficult one, even for Gotama. The scriptures were not concerned with historical accuracy; they wished only to record this great event in the most effective manner possible.

So, according to the oldest part of the Pali Canon, after his five friends left him in disgust, Gotama walked to the banks of the Neranjara river in search of a peaceful spot where he could meditate as he had done under the rose-apple tree in his childhood. Close to the village of Senanigama, Gotama noticed a leafy old pipal tree. It was the ideal spot, he decided, for his final meditation towards enlightenment. He sat down cross-legged under the spreading branches of the pipal in the meditative yogic position and vowed he would not move till he attained enlightenment.

Gotama sat in deep meditation all night. In the first watch of the night he gained knowledge of all his former births; in the second watch he gained the divine eye, the *dibbachakkhu*, which let him see that which the physical eye cannot see; in the last watch he understood the Chain of Causation, that is, how all phenomena, physical and psychic, are related to each other. As dawn came, the earth trembled and Gotama attained enlightenment. From that moment on he became a Buddha. He was thirty-five years old.

The Bodhi Tree

This is the name given to the pipal tree in Uruvela (modern Bodh Gaya) under which Gotama sat the night he attained enlightenment. The botanical name of the pipal is Ficus religiosa, which translates roughly as 'Sacred Fig'. The tree, a native of the Indian subcontinent, has distinctive heart-shaped leaves.

After Gotama's death, the pipal tree became a symbol of his presence, and an object of worship by Buddhists round the world. The original tree in Bodh Gaya was destroyed in the second century BCE, and the tree planted to replace it was destroyed in the seventh century CE. The tree that grows at Bodh Gaya today was planted in 1881 by a British archaeologist. It is believed to be a descendant of the original Bodhi tree.

It is said that the Buddhist nun Sanghamitta, daughter of King Ashoka who ruled India in the third century BCE, took a cutting from the original tree to Sri Lanka. She planted the tree in the temple at Anuradhapura, where it still grows.

Vajji

This was a confederation of several tribes of which the Licchavis and the Videha were the most important. Vesali was the capital of the Licchavis and Mithila of the Videhas. In Gotama's time, the Licchavis had become the most important tribe in the confederation, so that 'Licchavi' and 'Vajji' were used synonymously. The republic of Vajji lay north of the Ganga, east of Kosala and north of Magadha.

The strength of the Licchavis was their unity; they would stand by each other in both good times and bad. They are described as beautiful people, very wealthy and fond of bright clothes and riding in painted carriages, but also diligent and hard-working. They were also skilful archers. Many of the Licchavis were devout followers of Gotama's teachings.

The Ganga formed the boundary between the kingdom of Magadha and territory of the Licchavis; both states had equal rights over the river.

When Gotama visited Vesali, Bimbisara made a road five leagues long from Rajagaha to the river and the Licchavis did the same on the other side.

Vesali was one of Gotama's favourite destinations. His friend Mahali was from Vesali.

6 🪷 Spreading the Word: 528–508 BCE

Gotama remained deep in thought for several weeks after his enlightenment—the older scriptures say this period of contemplation lasted for four weeks, while the Jataka extends this to seven weeks. The scriptures recount how, as Gotama sat deep in meditation, two brothers called Tapussa and Bhalluka, happened to pass by; they were merchants, on their way to Rajagaha for trade. They saw Gotama sitting in meditation, and stopping, offered him some rice cakes and honey in a bowl to break his fast. Gotama accepted their offering, and though he did not preach to them, they became his first lay followers.

Gotama wondered what he should do with his new-found insights. Should he tell others of what he had discovered? Would they understand? What he had to say was so different, so new, and so completely against the beliefs of the day. Gotama then thought of his teachers, Alara and Uddaka. They were wise men, surely they would understand? But he learnt that they had died, Alara only seven days earlier. He then thought of his five friends, the Panchavaggiya monks; he knew they were staying at Isipatana near Varanasi and he set out to find them.

On his way to Isipatana, he met Upaka, an old acquaintance. Upaka noticed the change in Gotama, and asked what had happened to him. Gotama told of his awakening, but Upaka, incredulous and sceptical, refused to believe him, and turned away down a side road.

The five monks, who were living in a grove in Isipatana known as the Deer Park, were also slow in welcoming their friend and companion. After all, he had let them down by giving up the austere life. But, as Gotama drew near, they too became aware of a change in him, and despite themselves, sat down to listen to what he had to say. So, there in the Deer Park at Isipatana, Gotama explained for the first time the insights that had led to his enlightenment. It was the full moon day of the lunar month of *asalha*, the eighth month in the Indian calendar, which usually coincides with the modern month of July.

Gotama advised the five monks to follow the Middle Way, and to avoid the two extremes of self torture and self indulgence, for neither led to wisdom. He then explained the Four Noble Truths which, he said, were the following: the truth of suffering; its cause; its end; and the way to its end. The world, explained Gotama, was full of suffering; its cause was craving or desire; the end of suffering was the end of desire which came with Nibbana; the way to Nibbana was the Middle Way, or the practice of the Holy Eightfold Path. The Eightfold Path, continued Gotama, was made up of eight parts. These were: Right Understanding, Right Attitude, Right Speech, Right Conduct, Right Means of

Livelihood, Right Endeavour, Right Mindfulness and Right Meditation. Only when he had realized these Four Noble Truths and understood the practice of the Eightfold Path, said Gotama, did he attain enlightenment.

This discourse came to be known as the *Dhammachakkappavattana Sutta*, or the 'Setting the Wheel of Dhamma in Motion' sermon. It gives the essence of Gotama's 'dhamma' (the Pali term used by Buddhists to describe the teachings of Gotama). Gotama's teachings were not about blind faith, or worshipping any god; the way to Nibbana, believed Gotama, was through action. The practice of the Eightfold Path was fundamental to Gotama's teachings; he mentioned it in his first sermon, and it was also the last thing he spoke of as he lay dying in Kusinara forty-five years later. The world, said Gotama, was in a state of constant change; having once found the Middle Way, there was no guarantee that one would not lose it again. One had to strive for it constantly, and know that it was as unpredictable as life itself. Nibbana could not be reached through passive belief or worship; one had to work for it, and work for it constantly.

As the five monks listened to Gotama's sermon, there arose in Kondanna a joyful realization that Gotama's words made complete sense to him. His doubts disappeared and he became ready to follow Gotama's methods to Nibbana. He thus became Gotama's first disciple. By the end of his discourse, the other four monks were also convinced, and joined Gotama. This was the beginning of Gotama's Sangha, the Order of monks that he established.

A fully ordained follower of Gotama was called a *bhikku*. Though the literal meaning of the Pali word is 'one who begs', a bhikku did not beg, not in the manner in which we use the term today. Gotama's monks lived on the alms they were given, for which they would wait silently at the doors of their supporters. The bhikkus were not priests or mediators between men and gods. They lived a life of poverty and celibacy, but could leave the life any time they chose.

From this point on, Gotama's followers increased rapidly. He was joined first by Yasa, the son of a rich merchant of Varanasi, who became a monk. Yasa's father, who came searching for his son, also became a follower as did several members of Yasa's family. Four of Yasa's close friends, hearing that Yasa had become a monk, were so impressed that they came to listen to Gotama preach and stayed to join the Order. As the news spread, fifty more of Yasa's friends and acquaintances joined Gotama as monks.

Soon Gotama had sixty bhikkus in his Sangha. It was now time to spread the dhamma. Gotama told his sixty monks to travel and to teach the dhamma for the welfare of gods and men. The monks left, no two travelling in the same direction, and returned with many others wishing to join the Order. With the number of his followers growing, Gotama began to think of practical issues—how would he protect his Order and make sure that his dhamma would continue to spread? He realized that he would need powerful and wealthy supporters.

Gotama remembered the promise that he had made to Bimbisara, king of Magadha. He spent the three months of the rainy season at Isipatana, but as soon as the rains were over he set off for Rajagaha, the capital of Magadha. On the way he stopped at Uruvela where, along the banks of the Neranjara river lived the three ascetic brothers Uruvela-Kassapa, Nadi-Kassapa and Gaya-Kassapa (known as the Tebhatika Jatila), and their thousand followers. The brothers, at first sceptical, were finally convinced by Gotama's teachings, and joined his Order, as did their thousand followers.

Gotama finally reached Rajagaha with his large following of monks. Here Bimbisara, who was still king, came to meet him. Hearing him preach, Bimbisara became a follower of Gotama. He wanted Gotama and his monks to stay in Rajagaha, and so gifted to them the garden of Veluvana. Veluvana was ideal for the Order—it was a little way away from the town, yet not so far that it was not accessible to people; it was clean and free of the pollution of the city, and its quiet seclusion was perfect for Gotama and his monks. Gotama accepted the king's gift, and it is said that Bimbisara had a large house built there for the monks to live in. From that time on till his death thirty-seven years later, Bimbisara did all he could to help Gotama spread his dhamma, even setting a practical example to his subjects by observing the fasts recommended by Gotama.

Gotama stayed in Rajagaha for two months. It was during this period that he was joined by Sariputta and Moggallana, who went on to become two of his most trusted and important disciples. Both men were older than Gotama. They had been born on the same day in neighbouring villages close to Rajagaha, and having grown up together, they were close friends. While still teenagers, they had decided to renounce the world and had become followers of a well-known teacher called Sanjaya Belatthiputta. But they were not content with what they had learnt from Sanjaya. One day, Sariputta ran into Assaji, one of the Panchavaggiya monks, and was converted by him to Gotama's teachings. He repeated to Moggallana what he had learnt from Assaji, and Moggallana too became a follower. The two men left Sanjaya and joined Gotama, taking with them the five hundred other followers of Sanjaya.

Sariputta was wise and quick, and was soon able to explain Gotama's teachings as well as Gotama himself. Moggallana, through meditation, developed extraordinary psychic and mental powers. Moggallana used his powers only for good. It is said that once, when some monks were disturbing Gotama by their loud and frivolous chatter, Gotama asked Moggallana to give them 'a good stir'. Moggallana, by the power of his mind, managed to make the house shake, and the monks ran out in fear. Gotama then explained to them that they should spend their time in meditation as Moggallana had done, and develop the power of their minds. Both Moggallana and Sariputta died before Gotama. Sariputta, realizing that his health was failing and that he did not have long to live, returned home to his mother and died in peace. Moggallana was attacked and murdered by some thugs; wounded and hurt he managed to find his way to Gotama, and died at his feet.

Gotama was now firmly established at Rajagaha—he had the favour and protection of the king; his followers included young men like Yasa who belonged to some of the wealthiest families of the region; and even men from traditional Brahmin backgrounds like the Panchavaggiya monks, and established teachers such as the three Kassapa brothers, had willingly given up the old ways to be with him.

Of course, Gotama had his critics too. The people of Rajagaha, watching the number of his followers grow, became worried: if all the young men of Rajagaha became monks, what would become of the women? Who would their daughters marry? How would their families grow? But Gotama reassured the people, and gradually the protests died out.

Soon Gotama's fame spread to the neighbouring lands. The Licchavis sent his friend Mahali to invite him to Vesali, their capital. Vesali was in the grip of famine, and its citizens were dying of starvation and disease. It is said that after Gotama's visit and the sermon he preached there, the city became free of pestilence.

Meanwhile, Suddhodana, Gotama's father, heard that his son had fulfilled the prophecy and become a Buddha. He sent Kaludayi, Gotama's childhood friend and playmate, to invite him to Kapilavatthu. Gotama accepted his father's invitation and left for Kapilavatthu together with several hundred of his monks. This was his first visit home after his renunciation. Seven years had passed since he had stolen out of the palace that night, leaving behind his sleeping wife and their newborn son, Rahula. It was time for him to return and make his peace with them. His parents too, waited for him, still not completely accepting the path that he had chosen.

As he entered the city, members of his large and powerful family gathered to greet him. Gotama realized that they still looked upon him as their relative, and had not understood the change in him. It is said that he then performed a miracle to convince them of his powers, after which they acknowledged that he had indeed become a Buddha.

On the second day of his visit, Gotama picked up his bowl and went begging for food in the streets of Kapilavatthu. Suddhodana was deeply unhappy to see this, and protested that Gotama should not so demean himself and his family. But when Gotama explained that this was the custom of all Buddhas, Suddhodana accepted it. Listening to his son preach, he finally understood why Gotama had chosen to become a Buddha rather than a king, and became a convert to his ideas. Suddhodana died four years after Gotama's first visit to Kapilavatthu. As his father lay upon his deathbed, Gotama hurried to be with him; Suddhodana died in peace with his beloved son by his side.

Gotama's wife Bimba also saw him begging on the streets of Kapilavatthu. Unlike Suddhodana, she was neither angry nor unhappy at this; instead, she was overwhelmed by the grace and serenity on his face. But when he was invited to the palace for a meal, she refused to go with the other women to pay her respects to him. 'If I have any virtue in me,' she declared, 'let him come to me.' When Gotama heard this, he went to see her. 'Say nothing. Let her greet me as she wishes,' he ordered. Bimba fell at Gotama's feet, and holding them in her hands, put her head on them. Suddhodana, deeply moved by his daughter-in-law's reaction, told Gotama how she had lived like an ascetic since he had left. It is said that Gotama, touched, acknowledged her loyalty to him.

On the seventh day of his visit, as Gotama was leaving the palace after a meal, Bimba sent their son Rahula after him. 'That is your father,' she told him. 'Go and ask him for your inheritance.' This is probably the only passage in the Pali Canon where Gotama's wife is mentioned by name.

Rahula followed Gotama as he left the palace and did as his mother had said. He pulled on Gotama's robe and said, 'Give me my inheritance.' Then, looking up into Gotama's face, he added, 'Father, even your shadow is pleasing to me.' Gotama looked at his son and thought—my son is asking me for his worldly inheritance, but that is full of sorrow; better than that would be to give him what I have learnt. And Gotama asked Sariputta to take Rahula into the Order of monks.

Gotama's half brother Nanda, the son of Suddhodana and Pajapati, had also joined Gotama as a monk a few days earlier. Suddhodana had accepted it in silence. But he could not take Rahula's ordination so calmly, and made Gotama promise that never again would he take children into the order without their parents' permission.

Many other Sakyans asked to join the Order. The most important of these were his Gotama's cousins Devadatta, Ananda and Anuruddha. Devadatta rose to great importance in the Order, but later questioned Gotama's authority and even plotted to kill him. Ananda and Anuruddha were the sons of Amitodana, Suddhodana's brother. Ananda was devoted to Gotama, and for the last twenty-five years of Gotama's life, he was his personal attendant and right-hand man. Anuruddha, Ananda's brother, was also deeply attached to Gotama. He was present at Gotama's death at Kusinara, and noted the exact moment of his passing. He was the one who kept order amongst the monks in the immediate moments after Gotama's death, and played an important part in preserving his teachings when the First Buddhist Council was called.

Gotama's stepmother, Pajapati, had become a follower of Gotama upon his first visit to Kapilavatthu. After Suddhodana's death, she asked Gotama to accept her into his Order as a nun. At first Gotama refused, but when Ananda pleaded her cause, he gave in and agreed to establish an Order of nuns, or *bhikkunis*. This was a landmark decision and one which set Gotama apart from other religious and spiritual teachers of the time—never before had women been accepted as the spiritual equals of men. It was a brave step, for by accepting Pajapati and the hundreds of other women who soon joined her, Gotama had challenged the established social and religious norms of his times. Later, Gotama's wife Bimba also became a nun under Pajapati.

Gotama returned to Rajagaha with his new converts from Sakya. During this second visit to Rajagaha, it happened that Anathapindika, a wealthy *setthi* (banker) from Savatthi, had come to Rajagaha on a business visit. His real name was Sudatta, but, because of his generosity towards the poor and hungry, he was called 'Anathapindika', or 'one who feeds the destitute'. His wife was the sister of the setthi of Rajagaha, and when he arrived at his brother-in-law's house he found him preparing a meal for Gotama and his monks. The setthi's preparations were so lavish that Anathapindika thought that the king had been invited. No, said his brother-in-law; the feast was for an ascetic called Gotama and his monks. Surprised by the honour in which he seemed to be held, Anathapindika decided to visit Gotama.

Gotama welcomed Anathapindika courteously, and spoke to him about his teachings. Anathapindika, deeply impressed, became a follower. He invited Gotama and his monks to spend the rainy season at Savatthi. Gotama accepted his invitation, but said that he and his monks would need solitude. 'I understand, O Blessed One,' replied Anathapindika, acknowledging Gotama's implicit request for a place for his monks to stay at Savatthi. Anathapindika's invitation and Gotama's acceptance paved the way for Gotama to return to his own country of Kosala and set up a base in Savatthi.

His business at Rajagaha satisfactorily concluded, Anathapindika left for Savatthi, giving orders along the way for rest-houses, gardens and parks to be built in anticipation of Gotama's coming. He had rest-houses built every few miles all along the road from Rajagaha to Savatthi, and bore all the expenses himself.

In Savatthi, remembering Gotama's request for solitude, he looked for a suitable place near the city, and found the grove owned by Jetakumara. According to some accounts Jeta was the son of Pasenadi, king of Kosala; other accounts say that he was Pasenadi's brother or cousin. Anathapindika bought the grove from him for the exorbitant sum of eighteen crores, and spent a similar sum on constructing within it the famous complex known as the Jetavanarama. The complex consisted of cloisters for the monks, meeting halls heated against the winter cold, indoor spaces for exercise, toilets, bathrooms, storerooms and sheds. Leafy trees and well-tended lawns surrounded the living areas, wells and ponds were dug in the surrounding gardens, and walking areas were laid out. Prince Jeta gave all the timber required for the buildings, and spent the eighteen crores he had received from Anathapindika on building a fabulous multi-storeyed gateway to the grove. A mango grove lay on the outskirts of the park, and just outside was a playground for children who were always welcome into Jetavana for a drink of water. The main road to Savatthi ran past the complex, and tired travellers could enter to rest and recover.

Over time, Jetavana became Gotama's headquarters and the administrative centre of his Sangha. It also became a residential monastery occupied round the year rather than for only the three months of the rainy season. Gotama himself spent nineteen rains at Jetavana and delivered 844 discourses there, far more than he did anywhere else. The twenty years that Gotama spent at Jetavana were also the most peaceful and productive years in his teaching life.

The support of Anathapindika and Jeta helped to establish Gotama firmly in Kosala. In addition, he also had the patronage of his old friend Pasenadi, who was now king of Kosala. Bandhula, another old friend, and now chief of Pasenadi's army, was also a follower.

Even in his own country of Kosala, attempts were made to discredit Gotama. He was accused of the murder of Sundari, a young woman belonging to a rival ascetic sect, whose body was found buried in the grounds of Jetavana. Even the king, Pasenadi, became suspicious of him—till his spies overheard the murderers boasting of the deed. They had been hired by a rival ascetic group who wished to destroy Gotama's reputation. Gotama remained calm throughout the incident, firm in his belief that the truth would be discovered, as it soon was.

Gotama's ideas went against the established beliefs of centuries. His teachings did not rely on the idea of a Supreme God or gods who could rescue humanity from its sorrows; instead he believed that Nibbana lay within each person, and could be achieved by following the right path. He did not believe in the caste system and accepted women into his Order as the equal of men. Despite these revolutionary, even iconoclastic ideas, Gotama attracted the most powerful men of the time; kings, noblemen, military commanders and merchants came to listen to him and became converts. In the short space of twenty years his influence had spread across most of northern India—from the powerful kingdom of Magadha (modern Bihar) in the east, across the Indo-Gangetic plain through Kosambi (modern Uttar Pradesh), to his own country of Kosala at the Himalayan foothills and what is now modern Nepal. The growing community of his monks continued to travel, spreading his dhamma far and wide.

The North Road or Uttarapatha

This was the name of a great trade route that ran across northern India along the Ganga river all the way to the great Persian Empire to the west. The eastern end of the North Road was Tamluk, in what is now West Bengal. From here, the road continued along the Ganga, through the kingdom of Magadha via its capital city Rajagaha; it crossed the Ganga, connecting the lands of the Licchavis and the Mallas, to Savatthi the capital of Kosala. From Savatthi, it proceeded north-west to Kapilavatthu, and from there another 1,100 kilometres to Takkasila in Gandhara, modern Pakistan, which was then a part of the Persian Empire. From Takkasila it extended further west to Balkh in Central Asia.

The North Road was also the route that Gotama followed in his travels as the son of Suddhodana visiting the court at Savatthi, as a young man studying at the University of Takkasila, upon his renunciation from Kapilavatthu to Rajagaha, and later as the Buddha, spreading his dhamma across the land.

7 🪷 The Beginning of the End: 508–483 BCE

Very little is known of the last twenty-five years of Gotama's life. The only event that can be dated with any certainty before the last year of his life is the death of his friend and patron, King Bimbisara of Magadha. This occurred eight years before Gotama's own death, when Gotama was seventy-two years old, and Bimbisara sixty-seven.

Bimbisara, as we know, was married to Kosaladevi, the sister of Pasenadi. Her father, Mahakosala, gave her a village near Kasi as part of her dowry. Kosaladevi was Bimbisara's chief queen and also his most beloved; her son was Ajatasattu.

Ajatasattu was an ambitious young man, and easily led. He came under the influence of Devadatta, Gotama's cousin. Devadatta had joined the Sangha on Gotama's first visit home to Kapilavatthu, and had risen to a high place in the Order. Over the years, he had lost his spiritual focus, and had become worldly and ruthlessly ambitious. He resented Gotama's control of the Order, and tried to create an alternative power base for himself. So he approached Prince Ajatasattu who, impressed with his display of yogic powers, gave him his support.

This emboldened Devadatta, who then decided to seize control of the Sangha. In a large gathering at Veluvana in Rajagaha, Devadatta demanded that Gotama, who was now feeble and old, hand over control of the Sangha to him. Gotama refused—not because he himself wanted to retain control, but because he felt that giving the Sangha to a man as competitive, unprincipled and ambitious as Devadatta would go against the basic principles of his teachings. Devadatta left Veluvana, swearing revenge on Gotama.

Devadatta then went to Ajatasattu with a plan: why did he not take the throne from his aging father Bimbisara, while he, Devadatta, killed Gotama and took over the Sangha? Together they could wield complete control over Magadha and the surrounding lands. Ajatasattu agreed, but was caught as he slipped into the king's chamber to kill him. He confessed the entire plan to the king, including the role that Devadatta had played. Upon hearing of Devadatta's involvement, Bimbisara's security officers recommended that Gotama and his entire Order be put to death, but Bimbisara refused. Gotama, he said, had already disassociated himself from Devadatta. Saddened by Ajatasattu's attempt to kill him, and realizing how desperately his son craved the throne, Bimbisara abdicated in his favour. Ajatasattu felt no gratitude—to make sure that Bimbisara did not change his mind, he arrested, imprisoned and starved him to death. Kosaladevi, hearing of her husband's cruel death at the hands of their son, died of grief.

Bimbisara's death was the beginning of the end. It brought in its wake events that changed the political landscape of northern India, and directly affected Gotama and his Sangha. Ajatasattu was an aggressive and ambitious ruler, not afraid to resort to both war and trickery to achieve his ends. He now backed Devadatta in his attempt to take over the Order, and sent his archers to shoot Gotama. But the archers, upon seeing Gotama, put down their weapons and refused to kill him. Devadatta tried various other means to kill him—he hurled a great rock at Gotama which missed him, but splinters from which hurt his foot and he had to be taken to the physician Jivaka for his wound to be dressed; Devadatta also let loose an elephant, crazed by toddy, on a road that Gotama was expected to take, but Gotama managed to tame the animal.

Bimbisara's death also had repercussions in Kosala. Pasenadi, angered by Ajatasattu's criminal cruelty towards Bimbisara and grief-stricken by his sister's death, took back Kasi, the village that had been part of Kosaladevi's dowry. In retaliation, Ajatasattu declared war on Pasenadi. At first, Ajatasattu was victorious, but Pasenadi finally defeated him and took him prisoner. As a condition of his release, he made Ajatasattu promise that he would never resort to violence again. Ajatasattu promised, and as a sign of his friendship, Pasenadi gave him his only daughter Vajira in marriage, and gave to her the disputed village as part of her dowry.

This was also probably the point at which Ajatasattu withdrew his support of Devadatta. Frustrated and angry,

Devadatta then broke away from the Order, inviting other monks to join him, which some five hundred of the younger bhikkus did. Devadatta and his followers left Rajagaha for Gaya. Gotama, unwilling to accept this rift, sent Sariputta and Moggallana to reason with the rebel monks; all except Devadatta returned to Gotama. It is said that soon after this incident Devadatta fell very ill; he died before he could make peace with Gotama.

Gotama was now an old man, and these upheavals would have taken their toll on him. However, his last years were not to be spent in peace. It was not enough that he had lost his old friend Bimbisara; Pasenadi, too, was in trouble. It is difficult to establish the precise order of events, but it was during the last few years of Gotama's life that Pasenadi discovered the deception that had been practised upon him by the Sakyans by sending to him Vasabha, the daughter of Gotama's cousin, Mahanama, to be his bride. The Sakyans had hidden the fact that Vasabha's mother was a slave. Pasenadi had not suspected the Sakyans of deceit, and had accepted Vasabha as his bride in good faith.

Vasabha had given him one son, Vidudabha, whom Pasenadi had made his heir. Vidudabha had never visited his mother's home. When he was sixteen years old, he insisted that he be allowed to go to Sakya and meet his mother's family. Vasabha, after much argument, finally allowed him to go. Vidudabha was welcomed warmly by his grandfather Mahanama, and during his visit was treated with all the honour and respect due to a prince of his standing. On the day that he was to leave, one of his men overheard a remark made by a slave woman—she was washing with milk a seat that the prince had used, and grumbling that this was where the son of the slave woman Vasabha had sat. Vidudabha's man reported to the prince what he had overheard. Vidudabha, angry and humiliated, vowed that when he ascended the throne of Magadha, he would wash it with the blood of the Sakyans.

When Pasenadi discovered the truth about Vasabha's birth and realized how he had been fooled by the Sakyans, he flew into a terrible rage. He took away all royal privileges from Vasabha and her son, and reduced them to the status of slaves. Gotama, hearing of Pasenadi's anger, went to the palace to reason with him. Vasabha, he said, was the daughter of Mahanama, Gotama's own cousin and a man of noble lineage, while Vidudabha was Pasenadi's own flesh and blood. It was the father's family that mattered, said Gotama. Pasenadi gave in to Gotama's argument and forgave his wife and his son. At this time, both Gotama and Pasenadi would have been in their seventies.

Though immediate chaos had been prevented by Gotama's intervention, the consequences of this incident were severe and far-reaching. Vidudabha, once sure of his succession to the throne of Kosala, was now insecure. Both the prince and his father Pasenadi knew that the son of a slave woman would not be accepted easily as the future king. Whispers at the court implied that Gotama himself had been involved in the deception of the king. What's more, said the rumours, Mahanama's brothers

Ananda and Anuruddha were Gotama's right-hand men. It is at this point that we find Gotama moving once again to Rajagaha—perhaps the events at Savatthi had made it difficult for him to continue at Jetavana. This time in Rajagaha Gotama stayed not at Veluvana, but at the monastery built for him by his old friend Jivaka.

In Rajagaha, Ajatasattu was now firmly established on the throne. But racked by guilt for his father's murder and tortured by remorse, he had lost all peace of mind. He could not sleep because of nightmares, and became worn out with guilt and shame. At last Jivaka, who had continued as the royal physician even after Bimbisara's death, persuaded Ajatasattu to visit Gotama. He did so, nervous and trembling, afraid of Gotama's anger and expecting his monks to take revenge for his earlier support of Devadatta. Instead, Gotama received the prince in peace, and at the end of his visit, Ajatasattu became a follower of Gotama.

It was about a year later, while he was staying at the small Sakyan village of Medatalumpa, that Gotama met his old friend Pasenadi for the last time. Pasenadi came to see Gotama accompanied by the commander-in-chief of his army, Dighakaranya. Pasenadi handed Dighakaranya his sword and turban, and, while Dighakaranya waited outside, he went in to see Gotama. Pasenadi fell at Gotama's feet and kissed them humbly. He was no longer the proud and temperamental king of their youth, but a tired, sad old man who had lost his hold on his people and the respect of his ministers. Gotama, however, was still able to hold a crowd of hundreds with just the power of his discourse. Both men were eighty years old at this time and in the final year of their lives, but neither was to be allowed a quiet end.

When Pasenadi stepped out of Gotama's hut, he found that his commander Dighakaranya had vanished, taking with him Pasenadi's sword and turban, both symbols of royal power. He had left behind only a horse and a woman servant to look after him. The woman told Pasenadi that Dighakaranya was on his way to Savatthi to join Vidudabha who had risen in rebellion against his father. Dighakaranya was the nephew of Bandhula, Pasenadi's old friend and army chief whom he had had murdered unjustly. He had never forgiven the king for his uncle's death, and had now joined Vidudabha to overthrow Pasenadi.

Pasenadi realized that he could not fight Vidudabha or Dighakaranya on his own. His only hope was to go to his nephew Ajatasattu and seek his support. Pasenadi set off alone on the three hundred kilometre journey south to Rajagaha. After weeks of weary travel, he arrived at Rajagaha—only to find that the gates of the city had been closed for the night. The guards did not recognize him and refused to let him enter. Exhausted and worn out, Pasenadi took shelter at an inn outside the city gates. He died in his sleep, a lonely old man abandoned by the world. Ajatasattu, upon hearing the news, was deeply grieved. He insisted upon performing the last rites for his uncle, and conducted his funeral with great pomp and ceremony. He also wanted to attack Vidudabha at once, but his ministers advised that he should not.

Meanwhile, back in Sakya, Gotama also had his troubles. Vidudabha, determined to fulfil his vow of vengeance against the Sakyans for their deception, set out with the Kosalan army to attack Kapilavatthu. As he reached the border of Sakya, he saw Gotama waiting for him under a small tree. The shade of the tree was not enough to protect Gotama from the glare of the sun and Vidudabha suggested that Gotama sit under a nearby banyan. 'Don't worry about me,' replied Gotama, 'the shade of my kinsmen, the Sakyans, keeps me cool.'

Vidudabha, out of respect for Gotama, ordered his soldiers to retreat. Vidudabha marched against the Sakyans three times, and all three times he found Gotama waiting for him under the same tree. After the third time Gotama realized that he could not protect the Sakyans forever, and decided to return to Rajagaha. This was his last visit to the land of his childhood and youth. Vidudabha's army attacked Kapilavatthu, and though the Sakyans put up a spirited resistance, they were massacred, even the women and children. Mahanama was taken prisoner, but killed himself by plunging into a lake under the pretext of taking a bath.

On his way to Rajagaha, Gotama decided to stop at Vesali, the capital of the Licchavi tribe, where his disciple Sariputta was waiting for him. At Vesali a nobleman called Sunakkhatta, who had once been a follower of Gotama, denounced him to the Licchavi parliament. Sunakkhatta's chief complaint against Gotama was that he did not display any superhuman or mystical powers, that he was no different from ordinary mortals, and his teachings, based on reasoning and practical examples, led only to the end of craving. When Sariputta reported this to Gotama, the latter pointed out that by criticising him, Sunakkhatta had actually praised him. But Gotama did not stop long at Vesali, and continued to Rajagaha.

At Rajagaha, Ajatasattu was preparing for war against the tribal republics of the Mallas, Koliyas, Videhas and Licchavis who had entered into a defensive alliance with each other against Ajatasattu. The Videhas and Licchavis together made up the republic of Vajji, and collectively the tribes were known as the Vajjians. Ajatasattu was determined to defeat them and annex their territories. As part of his preparations for war, he was fortifying the village of Patali, which was located at the confluence of the Son, Gandak and Ganga rivers, and was therefore ideal for the launch of military expeditions. One morning Ajatasattu sent his prime minister, Vassakara, to tell Gotama about his plan, and to gauge his reaction. Ajatasattu wanted to find out whether Gotama believed that he could conquer the republics through war.

Gotama did not need any more conflict or war in his life—his old friend Pasenadi had just died a sad and lonely death, his own people, the Sakyans, were being massacred by Vidudabha, and now that he was back in Rajagaha, Ajatasattu was planning a bloody and brutal war. Pasenadi's death had completed the process that Bimbisara's death had begun—the old order had collapsed, giving way to a violent and aggressive world. The rising militancy of both Kosala and

Magadha threatened to change the world as Gotama had known it.

Gotama ignored Vassakara, and turning to Ananda, who was standing behind him, remarked that the Vajjians would remain strong as long they continued to hold their assemblies, lived together in harmony and respected their elders and the traditions of their ancestors. Vassakara interpreted this to mean that the tribal republics could not be conquered through war, but only by causing friction amongst them. In this way Gotama tried to avert another war and to prevent the republics falling into Ajatasattu's hands. He was not entirely successful—later Ajatasattu conquered the republics by sending Vassakara to sow distrust and discord amongst them, so that when Ajatasattu approached with his army, they could not put up a united defence and were easily defeated.

Gotama's comment to Ananda was true not only for the old republics, but also for the Sangha. In the aggressive and turbulent political climate of the day, the Sangha would not survive internal conflict or any lack of loyalty or solidarity by its members. The bhikkus had to remain steadfast in their beliefs. Concerned about the future of his monks, Gotama asked Ananda to summon all the bhikkus in Rajagaha to the hills outside the city. There Gotama asked them to hold regular assemblies, to respect the older monks, and to live in harmony with each other. He advised them to avoid the turbulence of the cities and seek instead the quiet of the forest, and to stay focused at all times on their practice of the Eightfold Path to Enlightenment.

Perhaps tired of the aggression he saw all around him, and realizing his utter helplessness to stop it, Gotama decided to leave Rajagaha for the last time. It was at this time too that Gotama lost his two most trusted disciples, Sariputta and Moggallana. From Rajagaha, Gotama left for Nalanda, and from there, taking only Ananda with him, he decided to return to his homeland, Sakya.

On the way he passed through the village of Patali, where Vassakara himself was overseeing the fortifications in preparation for war. At Patali, Gotama and Ananda were looked after with great respect by Vassakara. Gotama and Ananda however did not linger at Patali; they crossed the Ganga and hurried north to Vesali where Gotama wished to spend the rainy season.

As he approached Vesali, Gotama stopped at the village of Koti. The news of his arrival reached the city, and the courtesan Ambapali drove out to meet him. Ambapali had once been the mistress of Bimbisara and had a son by him. She listened reverently to Gotama preach his dhamma, and invited him to stay at her mango grove near Vesali, an offer that Gotama accepted. She also asked him to take his meal with her the following day. Just as Gotama agreed to do so, several Licchavi men arrived at the grove to invite him for a meal with them. The Licchavis were dressed in colourful clothes and jewels, and each rode a magnificent chariot. Gotama smiled when he saw them and remarked that the gods themselves had arrived. But he turned down their invitation, saying that he had accepted Ambapali's offer instead. The Licchavis did not mind, and returned to the city. Ambapali gifted her mango grove to Gotama and his monks, and later joined the Order as a nun.

Gotama, perhaps remembering Sunakkhatta's denunciation of him before the parliament of Vesali and not wishing to invite more conflict into his life, decided not to stay in the city for the rainy season. He moved to the village of Beluva, permitting only Ananda to stay with him. He dismissed all the other monks who had joined him from Vesali and the surrounding villages, asking them to find shelter where they could during the rains. This was unusual for Gotama—it seemed that he was weary of the world and was already preparing to leave it. At Beluva, he fell severely ill with sharp pains, and though he recovered, the illness left him weak and exhausted.

Ananda was deeply shaken by Gotama's illness. For the first time he realized that Gotama may die. But he had comforted himself with the thought that Gotama would not die before he had made some arrangements for the continuation of the Order. Gotama sighed and explained that he had taught the bhikkus all that he could, and now his work was done. He had never thought in terms of the Sangha being led, either by himself or any chosen leader—all bhikkus had the same knowledge, there was nothing that set one apart from the other. Each bhikku, said Gotama, must rely only on himself, and dhamma alone would be his refuge.

When the rains came to an end, Gotama asked Ananda to call his monks together. His end was near, he said, and he must bid them farewell. The monks assembled at Vesali, where Gotama addressed them. He urged them to follow the Eightfold Path and remain true to the dhamma. Next morning, he left Vesali, knowing that he would never see the city again.

Pataligama, Pataliputta

Located near the modern city of Patna in Bihar, Patali was just a village during Gotama's time. Its location, at the confluence of three great rivers, the Son, Gandak and Ganga, made it strategically important, and Ajatasattu fortified it as part of his preparations for war against the northern republics. Gotama prophesied that it would become one of the greatest cities of the world, but also foretold its destruction by fire and flood.

After Ajatasattu's death, Pataligama replaced Rajagaha as the capital of Magadha. It reached its zenith as the capital of the emperor Ashoka who ruled Magadha from 269 BCE to 232 BCE. Ashoka's empire covered almost the entire Indian subcontinent.

Pataligama was named after the Patali plant, a small tree that grows all over India and has medicinal properties.

The city was known to the Greeks as Palibothra.

8 ☸ Nirvana: 483 BCE

Gotama was accompanied on his final journey by his cousins Ananda and Anuruddha, the monk Chunda, and a monk from Kosala called Upavana. They travelled north-west along the North Road in the direction of Sakya. They travelled through Bhandagama, Hatthigama, Ambagama, Jambugama and Bhoganagara. We cannot identify any of these villages today. From Bhoganagara, Gotama and his monks went to Pava, which is today the modern town of Fazilnagar. Pava was about a hundred and twenty kilometres from Vesali.

At Pava, Gotama stayed with Chunda, a metalworker. Chunda invited Gotama and his monks to a lavish meal, where he served a special dish called *sukaramaddava*. There is much dispute as to what this dish was—some commentaries say that this was a dish of pork, while others argue that it was a dish of truffles. It seems that Gotama was suspicious of this dish the moment it was served. He insisted that the sukaramaddava be served to him alone, and refused to let anyone else eat it. When the meal was over, he told Chunda to bury the sukaramaddava since it was indigestible. Once again, scholars argue about the significance of this comment— perhaps, say some, this was a flippant comment on

Chunda's abilities as a cook, while others suggest that Gotama had realized that the dish was poisoned and by asking Chunda to bury it, he wanted to make sure that no one else would eat it. We will never know for certain whether the sukaramaddava was poisoned or not; however what is known is that night Gotama fell violently ill. He began vomiting blood and his body was racked by pain.

The Pali texts tell us that Gotama mastered his illness with a great effort of will and set off for Kusinara. On the way, he was forced to rest, and sat down under a tree by the Kakuttha river. He told Ananda that he did not have long to live and would die at Kusinara. A little later, he told Ananda to make sure that Chunda the metalworker was not blamed for his death.

Gotama was exhausted and in pain by the time they finally reached Kusinara. He asked Ananda to make a bed for him between two sal trees in a sal grove by the road. The Buddhist texts tell us that as Gotama lay down beneath the trees, they burst into flower and showered him with their petals. Gotama declared that a greater honour to him would be for his teachings to be followed. The Mallas of Kusinara, learning that Gotama lay dying in the sal grove, came to pay their final respects.

Gotama knew that he did not have many hours left to live, and gave Ananda instructions for his cremation. Ananda, heartbroken, began to weep. Gotama gently reminded him of what he had taught him—all things pass, said Gotama, and so it was inevitable that he would too. Ananda begged him not to die, not just yet, not in Kusinara which was nothing but a cluster of mud huts in the jungle, and not worthy of him. Gotama consoled Ananda again and told him how Kusinara had once been a magnificent city called Kusavati.

Later that night, as Gotama lay in the sal grove with only his monks for company, a wandering ascetic called Subhadda came asking to see Gotama. Ananda refused, but Gotama overheard them and called Subhadda to his side. Gotama then explained the Eightfold Path to him, and Subhadda became his last convert.

It was the full moon night of the month of Vaisakh. Gotama turned to his monks and said that if any of them had any doubts about his teachings, now was when they should ask him. When the monks remained silent, he said, 'All things decay and pass away; seek your salvation with diligence.' These were Gotama's last words. Soon afterwards, he passed away. He had attained Nirvana.

When the Mallas of Kusinara learnt of Gotama's death, they came in hundreds to honour him. Mallika, the aged widow of Bandhula, covered Gotama's body with her jewelled stole, and for seven days the people of Kusinara celebrated his Nirvana. But when they gathered to light his funeral pyre, it refused to ignite till the appearance of Gotama's chief disciple Mahakassapa, accompanied by five hundred monks. When the rains had ended, Mahakassapa had received word in Rajagaha of Gotama's illness at Vesali. Though he had left Rajagaha at once to be with Gotama, he had arrived too late.

Gotama's pyre burnt away completely; it left no cinders and gave off no smoke. The Mallas fenced it with their spears and continued their celebrations of Gotama's Nirvana for another seven days. We are told that at this time there appeared seven claimants for his relics including Ajatasattu, the Licchavis of Vesali, the Sakyans of Kapilavatthu, the Koliyas, the Mallas of Pava, a Brahmin from Vethadipa, and the Buli clan from the city of Allakappa. But the Mallas of Kusinara refused to share his relics. The others, indignant and angry, threatened war. At this point a Brahmin called Dona stepped into the breach. It was wrong, said Dona, to fight over the relics of the Buddha, who had been a man of peace. He suggested that the relics be divided into eight equal parts for the eight claimants. His suggestion was accepted, and he was asked to distribute the relics. Dona did so, and for himself, he kept the vessel which had been used to collect and distribute the relics. The Moriya tribe from Pipphalvana who arrived late, carried off Gotama's ashes. Ultimately, stupas were built over these relics. Two centuries later, the emperor Ashoka who became a follower of Gotama's dhamma, redistributed these relics over several thousand stupas. Today they are enshrined in various stupas across Asia.

Important Buddhist Sites in India

The four places most sacred to the Buddhists are:

Lumbini: located in the Himalayan foothills in what is now Nepal, the birthplace of Siddhartha Gautama

Uruvela: modern Bodh Gaya in the modern Indian state of Bihar, the place where Gautama attained enlightenment

Isipatana: modern Sarnath, a few kilometres from the city of Varanasi in the modern Indian state of Uttar Pradesh, where he preached his first sermon

Kusinara: modern Kushinagara in north-eastern Uttar Pradesh, where he attained Nirvana.

Other important Buddhist sites in India include

Don: near modern Patna, it is the place where the Brahmin Dona built a stupa to enshrine the vessel which had contained Gautama's ashes

Mathura: in western Uttar Pradesh, visited by Gautama, who did not like the town very much; a centre of Buddhism for nearly a thousand years, and a great centre of Buddhist art. Modern day Mathura is a busy and crowded city, and an important pilgrimage centre for Hindus.

Nalanda: in Bihar, 90 kilometres south-east of Patna, where Gautama met and converted Mahakassapa, and later the site of the great university of Nalanda. Gautama visited Nalanda often, and many of his important discourses were given here; the ruins of the university can still be seen.

Pataligama: later known as Pataliputra, modern Patna, in Bihar, the capital of Magadha after Ajatasattu's death, and the capital of the emperor Ashoka two centuries after Gautama's death; the site of the Third Buddhist Council; the ancient city was constructed mainly of wood.

Rajagaha: modern Rajgir, close to Nalanda, about 100 kilometres from Patna, the capital of Magadha during the reigns of Bimbisara and Ajatasattu, the site of many important events in Gautama's life; nothing remains of the original city, though the impressive ring of hills are still as they must have been in Gautama's day

Savatthi: also known as Sravasti, near the modern city of Lucknow, in Uttar Pradesh, the site of Jetavanarama, the monastery built for Gautama by Anathapindika and where he spent more than twenty years of his life; the ruins of Jetavana can be seen, set in landscaped gardens

Vesali: modern Vaishali in north-western Bihar, the capital of the Licchavis, and one of Gautama's favourite retreats

Kapilavatthu: also known as Kapilavastu, outside the modern village of Piprahwa, on the border of India and Nepal, the place where Gautama grew up; the ruins of the old town can still be seen

✦ Epilogue: After Buddha

The sayings of Siddhartha Gautama resound through the centuries. The world today is changing faster than ever before. Economic development and technology have brought with them prosperity and growth, but also uncertainty, war, environmental degradation and the exploitation of man by man. Gautama's teachings to shed greed and desire, to become free of ego and to embrace the world with compassion and kindness thus carry special relevance today.

The work to preserve his teachings began three months after his death with the summoning of the First Buddhist Council at Rajagriha. The story goes that when the Buddha died, his monks began to weep with grief. Only one old monk, the barber Subhadda (not to be confused with the ascetic Subhadda who was the Buddha's last convert) rejoiced. The Buddha had once refused food that Subhadda had ordered to be prepared for him, and he had waited all his life for an opportunity to criticise the Buddha. He called to the other monks to stop weeping and said, 'We are well rid of our teacher and his rules; we can now do as we like.' Mahakashyapa overheard these words of the old monk, and as soon as the celebrations around the Buddha's Nirvana had ended, he called upon all the senior monks to meet at Rajagaha, where he declared they would recite the Buddha's teachings and commit them to memory so as to preserve and pass them on to future generations. The recitation of the Buddha's dhamma at this Council formed the heart of what we now call the Pali Canon.

In the years following Gautama's death, the bhikkus of his Order began to disagree amongst themselves regarding some of the rules laid down by Gautama. About a hundred years after his death, the Second Buddhist Council met at Vesali to discuss these differences. This was a significant event, for at the end of the Council, the Order split into two groups—the Theravada School consisting of those who adhered closely to Gautama's original rules, and the liberals who favoured a less severe interpretation. The liberals called themselves the Mahasangha; they eventually evolved into the tradition known as Mahayana Buddhism. The less austere practices of Mahayana Buddhism made it easier for the common people to follow.

One of the most important events in the spread of Buddhism was the conversion of the Mauryan emperor Ashoka to Gautama's dhamma. Ashoka succeeded to the throne at Pataliputra in 269 BCE after a prolonged and bloody power struggle. He then devoted himself to the extension and consolidation of the Mauryan Empire, so that it covered almost the entire Indian subcontinent. His conquest of Kalinga (modern Orissa) in 260 BCE was particularly bloody. The destruction caused by the war filled Ashoka with remorse. He gave up violence and became devoted to the practice of dhamma. He took it upon himself to instruct his people in dhamma and to spread Gautama's teachings far and wide. He made a deep study of Buddhist scriptures and took tours called *dhamma-yatras* during which he travelled his empire, visiting the common people and instructing them in dhamma. He also spread Gautama's teachings through his edicts which he had carved on rocks and stone pillars that he erected throughout his empire. He sent missionaries to spread Gautama's teachings all over India and beyond. His missionaries reached as far as Egypt, Palestine and Greece.

Ashoka's son Mahindra and his daughter Sanghamitra took Gautama's teachings to Sri Lanka. They carried with them a branch of the original Bodhi tree, which was planted at the temple in Anuradhapura. The tree still grows there. The Fourth Buddhist Council was held in Sri Lanka in the first century BCE. It was at this time that the Pali Canon was written down for the first time. The Buddhist tradition followed in Sri Lanka was of the traditionalist school, the Theravada. Over time, this tradition died out in India, but continued to thrive in Sri Lanka, from where it spread to Burma, Thailand, Malaysia, Cambodia and Laos.

Gautama's teachings reached China in 67 CE. Legend says that the Chinese emperor had a dream which told him to send his men down the Silk Road, the trade route between China and the West; the Emperor did so, and his men returned with a picture of Gautama and a copy of one of his sermons. The first Buddhist community in China was established in 150 CE. The Mahayana Buddhism introduced from India was influenced by China's own religions and beliefs, so that very soon there emerged a branch of Buddhism that was Chinese in flavour. This form of Chinese Mahayana Buddhism spread to Korea, Japan and Vietnam.

Buddhism reached Tibet from India some time during the eighth century CE. Though it suffered a decline over the next two centuries, it became firmly established in the eleventh century CE. In 1578, the head of the Tibetan Buddhists was given the title of Dalai Lama. The present Dalai Lama is the fourteenth. Forced to flee Tibet in 1951, he now has his headquarters in Dharamsala, India.

Buddhism finally made its way to Europe in the nineteenth century. The colonial powers—England, France and Germany—became aware of India's and China's ancient past, and scholars began to learn Indian and Chinese languages and translate ancient texts. Societies and clubs for the study of Asian culture sprang up all across Europe, including some with an eager interest in Buddhism.

From Europe, the interest spread to America. American interest in Buddhism was further fuelled by the coming of thousands of Chinese immigrants during the end of the nineteenth century, and again during the Second World War. In the 1960s came immigrants from South-East Asia—today, almost 75 per cent of American Buddhists are of Asian origin.

So, what made Siddhartha Gautama so special that entire kingdoms wept when he died, and kings and princes quarrelled amongst themselves to do him honour? He was a mortal, a human being like you and me—so why did his followers come to believe that he was God? Why do we still want to read about him twenty-five centuries after his death? Why do his words still touch us and his teachings shine like a beacon for so many?

For his friends and followers, Gautama's teachings provided a refuge from the harsh cruelties of the world. Pasenadi came to him seeking counsel, and at the end reassurance and peace; Ajatashatru sought peace of mind, an easing of the guilt he felt for his father's murder; Angulimala achieved release from the horrendous anguish of life as a murderer. Gautama extended to all of them a fair and impartial compassion.

Gautama's true greatness lies in his humanity. As a young man, he was tortured by questions that most of us have asked ourselves at some point in our lives—why are we alive, what is the point of our existence? We can identify with his anguish, and his desire to search for a better, more meaningful life. What sets Gautama apart and makes him different from most of us is that he had the courage to search for the answers. He was not afraid to leave his safe and familiar world and step out into the unknown. And having found the answers he was seeking, he spent the rest of his life living by them. This took him close to divinity in the eyes of his followers—not because he had risen above his humanity, but because he had embraced it more fully than any of us have done, and by doing so had touched the divine.

Gautama himself did not believe that what he had achieved was unique. It could be achieved by any man or woman if they were willing to apply themselves with diligence. Through hard practice and experiment, he had found the Eightfold Path which had led him to Enlightenment and would lead him to ultimate Nirvana. This path, taught Gautama, could be followed by anyone, and would definitely lead to Nirvana. But he did not want his teachings to be taken on blind faith. He encouraged his followers to action, to find out by doing what worked best for them. Gautama's own life was an example of constant doing. For him, the way to Nirvana was a process, a journey, during which the traveller took on responsibility for his own life. Nirvana was not be had through blind worship of a god or gods, but had to be worked for on a daily basis, while living in this world.

The Buddha's teachings are rooted in reality. He does not deny the existence of suffering, or sorrow or grief or pain. Instead, the first step to spiritual growth is the acceptance of suffering, and to understand how it fills us and all beings. Only then can we transcend it, by conquering selfishness and desire. Shedding ego makes it possible to live in peace with pain. Detachment, said Gautama, makes us see the world clearly and embrace it with true compassion; when the mind becomes free it is also at its clearest. He did not ask his followers to leave the world; rather he asked them to engage with it more fully. Nor did Gautama believe in the harsh asceticism of traditional religion—the way to Nirvana was not through self torture. Gautama's teachings are all embracing. They demand commitment and discipline, but do so with grace and compassion. Anyone can follow the Eightfold Path in the degree that they wish to—as monks, nuns, or as ordinary lay householders. And in this idea—that salvation can be found by everyone, in this world—lies Gautama's greatest appeal.

TRIVIA
TREASURY

Turn the pages to discover more fascinating facts and tantalizing tidbits of history about this legendary life and his world.

WHAT HAPPENED AND WHEN

BCE

- **563**: the birth of Siddhartha Gautama, the future Buddha
- **542**: Bimbisara ascends the throne of Magadha
- **539**: Cyrus the Great of Persia conquers Babylon
- **538**: Pasenadi becomes king of Kosala
- **534**: the renunciation of worldly life by Siddhartha Gautama;
  Gotama's son, Rahula, is born
- **528**: Enlightenment of Siddhartha Gautama; from now on he is a Buddha
  The Buddha preaches his first sermon at Isipatana (Sarnath)
- **527**: death of Mahavira
- **491**: death of Bimbisara; Ajatashatru becomes king of Magadha
- **484**: death of Pasenadi; Vidudabha becomes king of Kosala and begins his campaign to slaughter and eventually annihilate the Sakyans
- **483**: Nirvana, the death of the Buddha at Kusinagara
  The First Buddhist Council is called at Rajagriha, and the Pali Canon is composed

- **482**: death of Vidudabha; soon after, Kosala annexed by Magadha
- **461**: death of Ajatashatru

IMPORTANT PLACES AND PEOPLE IN THE BUDDHA'S LIFE

The list below gives Pali names and terms as they appear in the book as well as their Sanskrit spellings.

Ajatasattu [Ajatashatru]

He was the son of Bimbisara, and the king of Magadha from 491 to 461 BCE. His mother was Kosaladevi, the daughter of Mahakosala and sister of Pasenadi, king of Kosala. He married Vajira, Pasenadi's daughter.

He succeeded Bimbisara, whom he had imprisoned, tortured and killed. During his reign Magadha became the largest and most powerful of the kingdoms of northern India. He was a devoted follower of the Buddha.

Ambapali [Amrapali]

A courtesan of Vesali, she was found as a baby by the king's gardener, abandoned under a mango tree in the king's gardens. The gardener named her Ambapali (from 'amba' which means mango, and 'pallawa' which means 'new leaves'). He took her to the city and brought her up. She grew into such a beautiful young woman that many young noblemen wanted to marry her. Finally, so that the young men would not fight over her, she was appointed courtesan. She had a son, Vimala-Kondanna, by Bimbisara, king of Magadha. Her son was a disciple of the Buddha. Hearing her son preach one day, she renounced the world and became a nun.

The Hindi writer, Acharya Chatursen, has based his novel *Vaishali ki Nagar Vadhu* on her life. The 1966 Hindi film, *Amrapali*, is also based, though very loosely, on her story; the actress Vyjanthimala plays Ambapali in the film.

Ashoka

The son of Bindusara, emperor of Magadha from 269–232 BCE. He became a convert to the teachings of the Buddha after his bloody conquest of the kingdom of Kalinga. He raised Buddhism to the level of a state religion and spread the Buddha's teachings across the length and breadth of his vast empire which consisted of almost the entire Indian subcontinent. He also sent missionaries to several countries to spread the Buddha's word.

Avanti

One of the four powerful kingdoms in northern India during the Buddha's time, with its capital at Ujjeni.

Ayojjha [Ayodhya]

An important city in the kingdom of Kosala

Baranasi

The capital of Kasi, the modern city of Varanasi

bhikku [bhikshu]

Literally 'one who begs', this is the term used for a fully ordained Buddhist monk

bhikkuni [bhikshuni]

A fully ordained Buddhist nun

Buddha

A title, not a proper name, given to one who has attained enlightenment. We use the term 'the Buddha' to refer to the historical Siddhartha Gautama only, but such was not the case in his times.

Champa

A city on the river of the same name. It was the capital of Anga and was known for its beautiful lake along which grew *champaka* trees (champaka trees are found all over India; they bear large white fragrant flowers in the summer). The Buddha stayed here many times.

Devadaha

The capital city of the Koliya tribe and the birthplace of Maha Maya and Pajapati. The Buddha stayed and preached there many times.

dhamma [dharma]

The Pali term used for the teachings of the Buddha

dibbachakkhu [divyachakshu]

The 'divine eye' which enables one to see the visible as well as the invisible

Gandhara

A kingdom in the north-west, in what is now Pakistan. Its capital was the city of Takkasila, the site of the famous university.

During the Buddha's time, Gandhara was part of the great Persian Empire. Its king maintained friendly relations with King Bimbisara of Magadha, and trade and travel between the two kingdoms was free and frequent. The king of Gandhara, Pukkusati became a follower of the Buddha, though the Buddha's teachings did not take root in Gandhara till after his death.

Gotama [Gautama]

The clan name of the Buddha, and the name by which he is referred to in the Pali texts

gotta [gotra]

The Pali term for 'clan name'. The gotta was used much as a surname is used today. The Buddha belonged to the Gotamagotta, i.e. to the Gotama clan.

Isipatana

Modern Sarnath, close to the city of Varanasi, the site of the famous Deer Park where the Buddha preached his first sermon to the Panchavaggiya monks. Isipatana is the name used in the Pali texts. It means the place where holy men (Pali: *isi*, Sanskrit: *rishi*) fell to earth.

Kapilavatthu [Kapilavastu]

A city in the foothills of the Himalayas, the capital of the Sakya tribe and the home of Siddhartha Gautama. It has been identified as the modern village of Piprahwa in northern India, close to the border of Nepal.

Kasi

A kingdom on the banks of the Ganga, with its capital at Baranasi. During the Buddha's time it had become a part of the kingdom of Kosala.

Kosambi

The capital city of the kingdom of Vatsa, it was an important halt for trade and traffic to Kosala and Magadha from the south and the west. Ananda suggested it as one of the cities that the Buddha could choose for his Nirvana.

Koti, Kotigama

A village near Vesali. The Buddha stopped here during his last journey; the courtesan Ambapali and several Licchavi noblemen came here from Vesali to pay him honour.

Kusinara

Modern Kushinagar, it was the capital of the Malla tribe, and the place of the Buddha's death.

Lalitavistara Sutra

A Sanskrit text composed perhaps in the third century CE. It describes the childhood and youth of Siddhartha Gautama. Amongst other incidents from the prince's life, the *Lalitavistara Sutra* also relates the story of Siddhartha's wedding to Gopa, the talented and accomplished daughter of another Sakya, Dandapani.

Licchavi

The most powerful of the republican tribes during the Buddha's time. Their capital city was Vesali, and they were one of the tribes that made up the confederacy of Vajji. They are often referred to as the Vajjians. They were a proud and prosperous people, fond of bright colours and ornaments.

Lumbini

A garden that lay between Kapilavatthu and Devadaha; the site of the Buddha's birth. The park lies in what is now Nepal, just across the border from India. It is now known as Rummindei. A pillar stands at the site of the garden, commemorating the visit of the Mauryan emperor Ashoka to Lumbini.

Magadhi

The language spoken by the people of Magadha, and probably the language spoken by the Buddha.

Mahakassapa [Mahakashyapa]

One of the most important of the Buddha's disciples, he was called Pippali, and was the son of a Brahmin, from a village in Magadha.

Pippali was immensely wealthy, but one day gave up all his possessions and renounced the world together with his wife. When he saw the Buddha, he prostrated himself before him and became his follower. He was called Mahakassapa from then on (there are no reasons given for the change of name). He could not be present at the Buddha's death in Kushinagara, but the Buddha's funeral pyre refused to catch fire till Mahakassapa arrived. After the Buddha's death, he called the First Buddhist Council at Rajagriha to preserve the Buddha's teachings and pass them on to future generations.

Mahinda [Mahendra]

The son of the Mauryan emperor Ashoka, and the brother of Sanghamitta. He became a Buddhist monk at the age of twenty, and travelled as a missionary to Sri Lanka, where he carried the word of the Buddha.

Malla

One of the important republican tribes, and their country.

During the Buddha's time, Malla was divided into two parts; one had its capital at Pava, the other at Kushinagara.

Moriya [Maurya]

A warrior clan, one amongst those claiming the relics of the Buddha. They arrived too late, and had to be satisfied with the ashes. Emperor Ashoka was of the Moriyan clan.

Nalanda

A town near Rajagriha in Magadha. The Buddha stayed and preached there several times. During the Buddha's time, Nalanda was a busy and prosperous town; however, it was not till later that it became a centre of learning and the site of the famous university.

Neranjara [Nilanjana]

A river along the banks of which lay the town of Uruvela. It was along the banks of this river that the Buddha spent the night of his Enlightenment. The Neranjara is identified with the river Nilanjana.

Nibbana [Nirvana]

The Pali term for the ultimate freedom from the cycle of birth, death and rebirth; it is the highest goal for all Buddhists.

Pajapati [Prajapati]

The daughter of Suppabuddha, and the sister of Maha Maya, also married to Suddhodana. After Maha Maya's death she brought up the baby Siddhartha Gautama. Her own son was called Nanda. After Suddhodana's death, she joined the Buddha and became a nun.

Pasenadi [Prasenajit]

The son of Mahakosala and the temperamental king of Kosala. His sister Kosaladevi was married to Bimbisara the king of Magadha. He was the Buddha's friend and benefactor. He was overthrown at the age of eighty by his son Vidudabha, and died a lonely death at the gates of Rajagriha.

Patali, Pataligama, Pataliputta [Pataliputra]

Modern Patna; during the Buddha's time, it was a village near Rajagriha, at the confluence of the rivers Gandak, Ganga and Son. It was fortified by Ajatashatru as defence against the Vajjians. Later, the capital of Magadha moved from Rajagriha to Patali. It became famous as Patlaiputta, the capital of the Emperor Ashoka.

Rajagaha [Rajagriha]

Modern Rajgir. During the Buddha's time, it was the magnificent capital of the kingdom of Magadha.

Saketa

One of the cities of Kosala, and one of the six most important cities during the Buddha's time. It is believed to have been founded by Dhananjaya, who went from Rajagriha to Kosala.

Sakya

The tribe to which the Buddha belonged. Their country, also called Sakya, was a republic, and lay at the foothills of the Himalayas. During the Buddha's time, the Sakyans paid tribute to the king of Kosala.

Sakyamuni

The 'sage of the Sakyans', one of the titles given to Siddhartha Gautama as the Buddha, since he belonged to the Sakya tribe.

Sanghamitta [Sanghamitra]

The daughter of the Mauryan emperor Ashoka, and the sister of Mahinda. She became a Buddhist nun when she was eighteen, and later went to Sri Lanka as a missionary, carrying a branch of the original Bodhi tree with her to Anuradhapura.

Sariputta [Sariputra]

The chief disciple of the Buddha. He is also called Upatissa, which was probably his personal name. He was born on the same day as Moggallana in a village near Rajagriha. His father was Vanganta and his mother, Rupasari. It was because of his mother's name that he came to be called Sariputta ('son of Sari'). In Sanskrit texts he is called Sariputra, Saliputra, Sarisuta, or Saradvatiputra. He was converted to the Buddha's teachings by Assaji.

Savatthi [Sravasti]

The capital of Kosala, and one of the great cities of northern India during the Buddha's times. It was also the location of Jetavana, the Buddha's chief monastery.

Siddhattha [Siddhartha]

The name given to the Buddha at his birth

Tipitaka [Tripitaka]

Literally, 'three' (Pali *ti*, Sanskrit *tri*), baskets (Pitaka). The Pali Canon, so called because when it was written down it was divided into three sections.

Uruvela

Modern Bodh Gaya. In the Buddha's time a small town on the banks of the Neranjara river, where for six years Siddhartha Gautama lived with the Panchavaggiya monks, practising the severest austerities in an attempt to seek enlightenment.

Vatsa

One of the important kingdoms of northern India. It lay south of Kosala. Its capital was the city of Kosambi.

Vidudabha [Virudhaka]

The son of Pasenadi by Vasabha. In revenge for the deception practised upon his father by the Sakyans who had given Pasenadi a slave woman as his bride, Vidudabha vowed to massacre the Sakyans upon his accession to the throne of Magadha. He overthrew his father, probably in the year 482 BCE, and launched a campaign against the Sakyans which virtually annihilated the tribe. He died soon after.

THE AGE OF THE BUDDHA

The sixth century BCE is a watershed period in Indian history: this is when, for the first time, we have definite evidence of historical events and personalities. Instead of having to rely on doubtful legends and even more dubious myths to reconstruct the past, we now have authentic records on which to base our understanding of history. Our main sources for this period are the Buddhist and Jain scriptures, which though not perfect as historical documents, still contain valuable references to the economic, social and political conditions of the time. These scriptures, composed independently of each other, often mention the same people, places and events, and thus confirm each other.

From Village to City

Techniques for the smelting of iron and the production of steel had been discovered. This led to the manufacture of improved, sturdier, sharper tools and farming implements, which helped farmers to cut down and clear the dense forests of the Gangetic valley and farm the fertile land thus opened up. More and more people moved to the Gangetic plain, and the area became densely populated. Since the land was highly fertile, farmers began growing more than they could consume—fruit, rice, wheat, millet, sesame—and to trade the extra they had for other goods. As trade increased, so did wealth, and the scattered farming villages of the earlier age gave way to busy towns and bustling cities. The most important of these new towns and cities were Savatthi, Saketa, Kosambi, Kasi, Rajagaha and Champa.

The ancient cities were lively vibrant places—people from all castes and walks of life, from all parts of the subcontinent, gathered there. They interacted freely, no longer bound by caste or custom. Traders and travellers from far-off lands brought new goods and new ideas with them. We also see the growth of urban culture as gambling, prostitution, pubs, theatres, became part of the landscape. This new lifestyle brought with it a new morality that questioned the old ways.

The cities were dominated not by the Brahmin priests or the warriors of earlier times, but by a new and increasingly powerful group of people—the merchants, businessmen and bankers who controlled trade and money and challenged the authority of both priest and king. Wealth was now measured in gold rather than in cattle. Rich merchants were wealthier than the king, and the king would often need to call upon them for help in financing a war or a project.

Emerging Monarchies

The political scenery was also changing. Earlier, northern India had been divided into small kingdoms and tribal republics. The Buddha's home, Sakya, was one such tribal republic. The Koliyas, the Mallas, and the Licchavis were some of the other tribes in the region. Each was headed by an elected leader who ruled the tribe with the help of an assembly or *Sangha*. The tribes were typically fiercely proud and jealous of their independence. So far, the tribal republics had remained relatively isolated and untouched by the religion of the Vedas (for example, there was no caste system in Sakya). With the growth of trade and trade routes, the isolation of these tribal republics soon ended. Kapilavatthu, for example, became a trading post on the North Road, the trade route that connected the cities of the Gangetic plain to the West. Traders and travellers brought in their wake the turbulence of the wider world, and gradually the tribal republics were taken over by the emerging, ambitious monarchies of Kosala and Magadha. By the time of the Buddha, Sakya had become tributary state of Kosala.

The only tribe that managed to retain its independence for some time was the Licchavi. It was a confederation of several tribes of which the Licchavis and the Videha were the most important. By the time of the Buddha, the Licchavis had become the most important tribe in the confederation.

South of the Ganga and to the west of Magadha lay the two kingdoms of Vatsa and Avanti. The capital of Vatsa was Kosambi, a city of some importance because it lay at a critical point on the trade route to Kosala and Magadha. Ananda mentions this city as a place suitable for the Buddha's Nirvana. The kingdom of Avanti lay to the west of Vatsa, with its capital at Ujjeni.

To the north-west of the Gangetic plain lay the vast empire of the Persian emperor Cyrus the Great. He ruled Persia from 558 to 530 BCE. Cyrus the Great came to the throne sixteen years before Bimbisara, and in a few years, built the greatest empire the world had yet seen, extending from the Mediterranean Sea in the west to the Indus river in the east. His empire included the kingdom of Gandhara. The capital of Gandhara was Takkasila, the site of the famous university where the Buddha had probably studied as a young man.

CONTEMPORARIES OF THE BUDDHA, OTHER GREAT TEACHERS AND PHILOSOPHERS

In India

All over the Gangetic plain, people found the old ways of life falling apart. The world was changing far too rapidly for them to keep pace. The old religion of the Vedas no longer provided all the answers, and people everywhere were in a state of intellectual and spiritual discontent. This led to a great movement towards asceticism, as the best and the brightest left their homes and their families in search of answers. Hundreds of monks, sages, mystics and philosophers roamed the valley of the Ganga, seeking answers to the universal questions of life and liberation from its ills.

Vardhamana Mahavira (599–527 BCE)

A contemporary of the Buddha's, he is generally regarded as the 'founder' of Jainism. There are many references to the Jains in the Pali Canon. They were not on friendly terms with Gotama and his followers, and regarded them as their rivals. One incident that bears this out is the death of Moggallana at the hands of thugs hired by some Jains.

Gotama served as a disciple under two other great teachers, Alara Kalama and Uddaka Ramaputta. Some, like Sanjaya Belatthiputta, opposed him; others, like the ascetic Kassapa brothers of Uruvela, joined him.

Around the world

Interestingly, the discontent and dismay felt by the people of the Gangetic plain was not unique to them. During this period, people all over the world felt a similar disillusionment with their old beliefs, and the greatest minds of the time engaged themselves in the search for answers and great thinkers, philosophers and religious teachers appeared all over the world:

In China, **Lao Tzu**, the founder of Taoism, and **Confucius** (551–479 BCE);

In Iran, the prophet **Zoroaster**, the founder of Zoroastrianism, the faith of the Parsis of India;

In Greece, **Socrates** (469–399 BCE) and **Plato** (427–327 BCE) who encouraged the Greeks to think for themselves and accept nothing on faith.

THE BUDDHA IN ART

The Buddha had never wanted to be worshipped as a god, and therefore never encouraged his followers to make images of him. But his followers felt his death keenly, and after his passing, they sought ways to represent his life, his glory and their veneration for him. Slowly, representations and symbols of the Buddha found their way into art, sculpture and architecture.

Stupas

The Buddha's relics were enshrined in stupas [in Pali: *thupa*]. These were simple, dome-shaped structures built of mud and earth, used to house the earthly remains of kings and great men. Very early in the development of Buddhist art, stupas came to represent the Buddha's enlightened mind and his journey towards it, and became more complex in their structure and construction.

The earliest examples of Buddhist art that we find date back to the second century BCE, when stone replaced perishable wood, bamboo and clay as the preferred material for construction. Artists and sculptors also began to work in stone, the durability of which ensured that their work survived over the centuries. During this

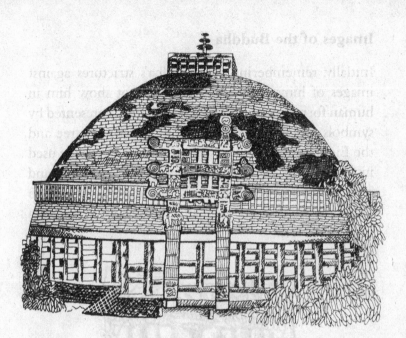

period stone railings and gateways began to be added to stupas. The railings and gateways were often densely and elaborately carved with scenes from the life of the Buddha.

The Great Stupa at Sanchi

This was originally built by Emperor Ashoka in the third century BCE. It was later enlarged and added on to by later kings. It is one of the oldest and most impressive of the Buddhist monuments that exist in India today. It is 120 feet across (36.6 metres) and 54 feet high (16.46 metres).

Images of the Buddha

Initially, remembering the Buddha's strictures against images of himself, his followers did not show him in human form. Instead, we see the Buddha represented by symbols, the most common being the Bodhi tree and the Eight-spoked Wheel. Other symbols that were used included a pair of footprints, an empty throne, a lion and a begging bowl. These symbols continued to be used to represent the Buddha, even after he began to be shown in human form.

The Buddhapada, or Buddha's Footprints from the Great Stupa at Amravati, 1st century BCE

Buddha in Gandhara and Mathura schools of art

Representations of the Buddha in human form first appeared in the first century CE in Gandhara. Images of the Buddha from Gandhara show him as a handsome prince, dressed in heavy, flowing robes and sandals; he is depicted with wavy hair, sometimes with a moustache, and often wearing jewelled ornaments. The statues are of stone or stucco. This school of art, known as the Gandhara School, shows heavy Greek influence

During the same period, another school of art emerged in Mathura. This presented a different image

of the Buddha—his robe was of fine muslin, draped over his right shoulder leaving the left shoulder bare. The Mathura School also added symbols such as the wheel on the palms of his hands.

During the Golden Age of Gupta rule, from the fourth to the sixth century CE there emerged the concept of the 'ideal image' of the Buddha. This was based on specific measurements that were considered to be, in the Buddhist canon, the ideal physical proportions of the perfect man, i.e. the Buddha. In these proportions could be seen the harmony and beauty of the Buddha's form. The Gupta school of art combined the characteristics of both the Gandhara and Mathura school of art, resulting in graceful and spiritually-inspiring images of the Buddha.

By the tenth century CE, Buddhist art began dying out in India. But as the Buddha's teachings spread outwards from India, so did the art and images. Each land that adopted the word of the Buddha also created its own art and imagery around him.

The Buddha in other lands

The Emerald Buddha in the Wat Phra Kaew, or Temple of the Emerald Buddha; Bangkok, Thailand

Carved out of jade and dressed in golden robes, this is one of the oldest statues of the Buddha in the world. According to legend, this was made in 43 BCE in Pataliputra, where it remained for 300 years. It was taken to Sri Lanka in the fourth century CE, and eventually reached Thailand. It was enshrined in the present temple in 1779.

The Buddhas of Bamiyan, Afghanistan

These were two giant statues of the Buddha, 53 metres and 38 metres in height, carved into the side of a cliff above the town of Bamiyan in Afghanistan. The statues were carved between the second and fifth centuries CE. They were in the Indo-Greek style of the Gandhara school, and were painted in gold and bright colours. In March 2001 they were condemned as 'idols' by the Taliban government of Afghanistan and destroyed.

The Giant Buddha of Leshan, Sichuan, China

71 metres high, this is the biggest carved stone statue of the Buddha in the world. It represents Maitreya, one of the Bodhisattvas, or the Buddha's incarnations in a former life. The statue took almost a hundred years to carve—it was begun in 713 CE and completed in 803 CE.

Gal Vihara, Polonnaruwa, Sri Lanka

Gal Vihara is a rock temple in the ancient city of Polonnaruwa. It was constructed in the twelfth century CE by Parakramabahu, king of Sri Lanka. The focus of the temple is four massive statues of the Buddha carved on to a granite rock face. The most impressive of these stone statues is the 14 metre long figure of the Buddha in a reclining position.

BUDDHISM TODAY

It is estimated that there are about 350 million Buddhists in the world today. This makes Buddhism the fourth largest religion in the world after Christianity, Islam and Hinduism. Today Buddhism is practised mainly in Asia, though there are a small number of Buddhists in Europe, the USA and Australia as well. Three main schools of Buddhism survive:

The Theravada

This form is close to the Buddha's original teachings and believes that enlightenment and nirvana are attained through an individual's own efforts with the help of dhamma. Theravada Buddhism is the form practised in Sri Lanka, Burma, Thailand, Laos and Cambodia. This is often called Southern Buddhism.

The Mahayana

This moved away from the Buddha's teachings, allowing the worship of divine beings called Bodhisattvas, supposedly the Buddha in his previous lives. Mahayana Buddhism is practised in China, Japan, Korea and Vietnam. This is sometimes called Eastern Buddhism.

Vajrayana

This form is considered by some scholars to be another form of Mahayana Buddhism. Followers of Vajrayana Buddhism believe that their version is the purest form of the Buddha's teachings, which he did not make known to his followers because it was too advanced for most of them. The oldest available Vajrayana texts date back to the fourth century CE; they were written at the university of Nalanda in Magadha. This form of Buddhism is practised in Tibet, Mongolia and parts of Nepal and Himalayan India. It is also called Tibetan or Northern Buddhism.

SOME BOOKS ABOUT THE BUDDHA

Buddha by Karen Armstrong (Phoenix, London, UK, 2002)

Confessions of a Buddhist Atheist by Stephen Batchelor (Spiegel & Grau, New York, USA, 2010)

Gem in the Lotus: The Seeding of Indian Civilization by Abraham Eraly (Phoenix, London, UK, 2005)

A Spoke in the Wheel by Amita Kanekar (Harper Collins. India, 2005)

Dictionary of Pali Names by G.P. Malalasekera (Motilal Banarasidas, India, 2006)

THE BUDDHA ON THE INTERNET

An excellent and accurate source of information about the Buddha is the Buddhanet website at http://www.buddhanet.net/e-learning/buddhism/lifebuddha/index.htm

Another reference source is the online *Buddhist Dictionary of Pali Proper Names*. This is based on the *Dictionary of Pali Names* by G.P. Malalasekera, which is available as printed version from The Pali Text Society,

London at http://www.palikanon.com/english/pali_
names/dic_idx.html

SOME FILMS ABOUT THE BUDDHA

Buddhadev, a silent film by Dadasaheb Phalke, 1923
Gotoma the Buddha, documentary, produced by Bimal
  Roy, directed by Rajbans Khanna, 1957
Little Buddha, by Bernado Bertolucci, 1993
Phra Puttajao (The Life of Buddha), 2D animation film,
  Thailand, 2007
Buddha, anime film based on the manga series *Buddha*
  by Osamu Tezuka, Japan, 2011